RUTH BELL GRAHAM

A QUIET KNOWING

CHRISTMAS

A Joyful Celebration of the Season

W PUBLISHING GROUP™

www.wpublishinggroup.com

A Division of Thomas Nelson, Inc.
www.ThomasNelson.com

Published by W Publishing Group, a Division of Thomas Nelson, Inc.

P. O. Box 141000, Nashville, Tennessee 37214.

Unless otherwise indicated, Scripture quotations are from

The King James Version of the Bible.

Other Scripture references are from the following sources:

The Holy Bible, New International Version (NIV). Coyright 1973, 1978, 1984

by International Bible Society. Used by permission of Zondervan Bible Publishers.

The New King James (NKJV). Copyright 1979, 1980, 1982, Thomas Nelson, Inc., Publishers.

Library of Congress Cataloging-in-Publication Data

Graham, Ruth Bell.
   A quiet knowing Christmas / by Ruth Bell Graham.
     p. cm.
   ISBN 0-8499-1762-X (hardcover)
   1. Christmas. I. Title.
   GT4985 .G714 2002
   263'.915—dc21

                        2002012897

Visit ruthbellgraham.com with ideas you'd like to see considered for

another QUIET KNOWING CHRISTMAS collection.

Printed in the United States of America

02 03 04 05 06 PHX 9 8 7 6 5 4 3 2 1

TABLE OF CONTENTS

An Introduction

When you think of Christmas, what first comes to mind? A beautifully decorated tree, tasty foods, brightly wrapped gifts, music, candles, family gatherings, shopping, filling stockings, perhaps sitting on Santa's knee, the manger?

For me, at my age, it is mostly memories of all the above. Happy, fun-filled memories. Some of my memories include the reading of Christmas stories. Reading has played a major role in my life from the time I was a small girl living in China. Each evening, we all gathered in the living room, and while the women did hand work, the men took turns reading out loud to us. One of my most cherished Christmas memories is listening to Daddy read *Why the Chimes Rang*.

Christmas is a special time of year, but so much of its specialness is lost in the hustle and bustle of the seasons. I put this book together to encourage families to spend time together reading, preparing a tasty Christmas treat, or perhaps making a Christmas craft. As we began to select the stories that would be included, I wanted some of my old favorites, but I began to discover stories that are destined to become new favorites. I trust that you and your family will enjoy them as much we do.

Have a very Merry Christmas.

—RUTH BELL GRAHAM
LITTLE PINEY COVE, NORTH CAROLINA
SUMMER 2002

A QUIET KNOWING CHRISTMAS

CHAPTER ONE

A Glory Beheld

A Quiet Knowing Christmas

*A*nd it came to pass in those days, that there went out a decree from Caesar Augustus, that all the world should be taxed. . . . And all went to be taxed, every one into his own city. And Joseph also went up from Galilee, out of the city of Nazareth, into Judaea, unto the city of David, which is called Bethlehem; (because he was of the house and lineage of David:) to be taxed with Mary his espoused wife, being great with child.

And so it was, that, while they were there, the days were accomplished that she should be delivered. And she brought forth her firstborn son, and wrapped him in swaddling clothes, and laid him in a manger; because there was no room for them in the inn.

And there were in the same country shepherds abiding in the field, keeping watch over their flock by night. And, lo, the angel of the Lord came upon them, and the glory of the Lord shone round about them: and they were sore afraid.

And the angel said unto them, Fear not: for, behold, I bring you good tidings of great joy, which shall be to all people. For unto you is born this day in the city of David a Saviour, which is Christ the Lord. And this shall be a sign unto you; Ye shall find the babe wrapped in swaddling clothes, lying in a manger.

And suddenly there was with the angel a multitude of the heavenly host praising God, and saying, Glory to God in the highest, and on earth peace, good will toward men.

And it came to pass, as the angels were gone away from them into heaven, the shepherds said one to another, Let us now go even unto Bethlehem, and see this thing which is come to pass, which the Lord hath made known unto us. And they came with haste, and found Mary, and Joseph, and the babe lying in a manger. And when they had seen it, they made known abroad the saying which was told them concerning this child. And all they that heard it wondered at those things which were told them by the shepherds.

But Mary kept all these things, and pondered them in her heart.

—LUKE 2:1, 3–19

*N*ow when Jesus was born in Bethlehem of Judaea in the days of Herod the king, behold, there came wise men from the east to Jerusalem, saying, Where is he that is born King of the Jews? for we have seen his star in the east, and are come to worship him.

When Herod the king had heard these things, he was troubled, and all Jerusalem with him. And when he had gathered all the chief priests and scribes of the people together, he demanded of them where Christ should be born. And they said unto him, In Bethlehem of Judaea: for thus it is written by the prophet, And thou Bethlehem, in the land of Juda, art not the least among the princes of Juda: for out of thee shall come a Governor, that shall rule my people Israel.

Then Herod, when he had privily called the wise men, inquired of them diligently what time the star appeared. And he sent them to Bethlehem, and said, Go and search diligently for the young child; and when ye have found him, bring me word again, that I may come and worship him also.

When they had heard the king, they departed; and, lo, the star, which they saw in the east, went before them, till it came and stood over where the young child was. When they saw the star, they rejoiced with exceeding great joy.

And when they were come into the house, they saw the young child with Mary his mother, and fell down, and worshipped him: and when they had opened their treasures, they presented unto him gifts; gold, and frankincense, and myrrh. And being warned of God in a dream that they should not return to Herod, they departed into their own country another way.

—MATTHEW 2:1-12

THOSE WERE NO ORDINARY SHEEP

*Y*ears ago, I read the following in *The Life and Times of Jesus the Messiah* by Alfred Edersheim:

Jewish tradition may here prove both illustrative and helpful. That the Messiah was to be born in Bethlehem was a settled conviction. Equally so was the belief, that He was to be revealed from *Migdal Eder*, "the tower of the flock." This *Migdal Eder* was not the watch-tower for the ordinary flocks which pastured on the barren sheep-ground beyond Bethlehem, but lay close to the town, on the road to Jerusalem. A passage in the *Mishnah* leads to the conclusion that the flocks which pastured there were destined for Temple sacrifices, and, accordingly, that the shepherds who watched over them were not ordinary shepherds. The latter were under the ban of Rabbinism, on account of their necessary isolation from religious ordinances, and their manner of life, which rendered strict legal observance unlikely, if not absolutely impossible. . . . Of the deep symbolic significance of such a coincidence, it is needless to speak.

I was so touched by the fact that these were no ordinary sheep, I wrote the following:

Those were no ordinary sheep . . .
no common flocks,
huddled in sleep
among the fields,
the layered rocks,
near Bethlehem
That Night;
but those
selected for the Temple sacrifice:
theirs to atone for sins
they had not done.

How right
the angels should appear
to them
That Night.

Those were no usual shepherds
there, but outcast shepherds
whose unusual care
of special sheep
made it impossible to keep
Rabbinic law,
which therefore banned them.

How right
the angels should appear
to them
That Night.

—RUTH BELL GRAHAM

*G*od decided to make the arrival of His Son startlingly different from what the world expected. So, the night of His Son's birth, He sent a heavenly host of angels to announce the birth to humble shepherds on a hillside in Judaea. What a present for them!

The world expected the Christ to arrive in a scene of dazzling splendor, like a king from heaven. But no, God planned it otherwise. He made the scene of the nativity radiant with the simplicity of a lowly manger, with Joseph, the husband of Mary, and the shepherds, and the beasts of burden in the stalls round about. Instead of princely robes of velvet and satin, our Lord was wrapped in swaddling clothes, and He lay in a bed of straw.

—Dale Evans Rogers
from Christmas Is Always

*L*ate, very late, there was a commotion outside. Men were shouting and running, their sandals scuffing on the dirt. Aaron poked Anna, his finger on his lips. Quietly, the children jumped to their feet and ran to the door.

They stared at the men talking so loudly in the middle of the night. Not only their shaggy hair and ragged robes but also their smell marked them as shepherds. Probably the outcast shepherds who kept watch over the sheep outside Bethlehem––the sheep chosen for the temple sacrifices.

But what were they saying? They had seen an angel?

Aaron looked at them again to make sure they were really shepherds and not crazy people. "We saw an angel!" they repeated. "And the angel told us about a baby being born in Bethlehem—a baby called 'Savior' and 'Lord.'" They had just seen the baby with their own eyes! He was in a cave that the innkeeper used for a stable.

—Ruth Bell Graham
from One Wintry Night

Angelic Cream Twists—German Cookies
with a Heavenly Taste

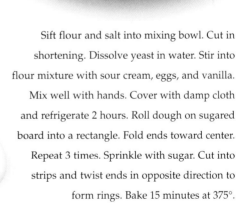

3 ½ cups flour

1 teaspoon salt

1 cup shortening

1 package dry yeast

¼ cup lukewarm water

¾ cup sour cream

2 whole eggs

1 cup sugar

1 teaspoon vanilla

Sift flour and salt into mixing bowl. Cut in shortening. Dissolve yeast in water. Stir into flour mixture with sour cream, eggs, and vanilla. Mix well with hands. Cover with damp cloth and refrigerate 2 hours. Roll dough on sugared board into a rectangle. Fold ends toward center. Repeat 3 times. Sprinkle with sugar. Cut into strips and twist ends in opposite direction to form rings. Bake 15 minutes at 375°.

—MARTHA WIEBE

THE SHEPHERD'S DOG

Out on the windy hill
Under that sudden star
A blaze of radiant light
Frightened my master.

He got up, left our sheep,
Tramped over the moor.
And I, following,
Came to this open door,

Sidled in, settled down,
Head on my paws,
Glad to be here, away
From the wind's sharpness.

Such warmth is in this shed,
Such comfort from this Child,
That I forget my hard life,
Ignore the harsh world,

And see on my master's face
The same joy I possess,
The knowledge of peace,
True happiness.

—LESLIE NORRIS
FROM *NORRIS'S ARK*

Bethlehem Was Never As Miserable As This!

The holiday season had arrived again, brimming with joy and anticipation. But there was also the usual hustle and bustle of all the preparations—shopping, wrapping, decorating, and baking.

Finally everything was ready. We loaded into the car, and Stephan, the children, and I drove to my parents' home in North Carolina. That first glimpse of "home" always fuels our excitement and anticipation. It's almost as though we can smell the fresh apple pie and feel the warmth of a cozy fire before we get out of the car.

The excitement built to a crescendo on Christmas Eve as each child and adult hung his or her stocking from the fireplace mantle in the large living room. With a twinkle in his eye, Daddy gathered all of us around and placed a long distance call to Santa at the North Pole— just to make sure he'd received all the children's gift lists and to wish him a speedy trip.

As we tucked the children into bed, the unmistakable sound of sleigh bells jingled somewhere over the roof of the house — my brother had hung donkey bells on the chimney. Needless to say, sleep didn't come easily for the children that night!

When Christmas morning arrived, everyone rushed downstairs. A fire blazed merrily on the hearth, and the aroma of coffee and sweet rolls met us in the kitchen. By strict family tradition, no one is allowed into the living room where the Christmas tree stands guard over the bulging stockings and brightly wrapped gifts until after breakfast.

The children quickly inhaled a few bites and then sat waiting as patiently as possible.

Finally the last drop of coffee was downed, and the eager faces of the children turned for the anticipated permission to rush into the living room.

But Daddy wanted to have devotions first. He announced that he would read the Christmas story. The children accepted this with a few audible sighs. Then, after the story and prayer, they jumped up out of their seats.

But once again they were disappointed. This time, my sister, Anne, suddenly said she wanted the children to line up and enter the living room one by one so she could take pictures.

That did it! My five-year-old son turned to his grandmother and said with utter exasperation and disgust, "Bethlehem was never as miserable as this!"

Later, smiling as I recalled my son's remark, I remembered another Christmas Eve when I sat on the floor with tears of exhaustion streaking down my cheeks, wrapping gifts until long past midnight. My smile faded as I remembered just how miserable I'd felt that night. Something has happened to our holiday season that often makes it seem more of a burden than a blessing.

Have you ever wondered how that first Christmas Eve might have been celebrated? Were the cherubim and the seraphim, angels of every description, hurriedly preparing to send the Lord of heaven down to earth in the form of a baby boy?

Perhaps on one side of heaven angels were working on the magnificent program they would present to the shepherds. Another angel might have been arranging to send that special star sailing across the skies to eventually guide the wise men to the little Messiah. Maybe another angel tenderly watched over Joseph and Mary as they made their way toward the stable.

Of course we don't know exactly what happened, but we do know that when all was ready, "God sent forth his Son" (Galatians 4:4). And all of heaven gathered as the King of kings and Lord of lords laid aside His glory, placing it at His Father's feet and saying, "A body hast thou prepared me. . . . Lo, I come . . . to do thy will, O God" (Hebrews 10:5, 7).

While the heavenly preparations might have been complex, the earthly men and women involved in the first Christmas kept it simple.

The hearts of a few willing people—Mary, Joseph, the shepherds, the wise men—were simple. The site of the birth, a small stable in a small town, was simple. The celebration was simple: shepherds, hard-working men, left their work for a few hours to go and "see this thing which [had] come to pass" (Luke 2:15). And then they returned to their responsibilities.

The gifts were also simple, yet their value was priceless, timeless, and eternal: Joseph gave his obedience, Mary her body, the shepherds brought adoration, and the wise men gave their worship.

But then there were those who missed that first Christmas altogether: The innkeeper was too busy with the mundane cares of his guests. The guests themselves were too concerned with bodily comforts and personal affairs to be bothered with happenings in the stable. King Herod was too absorbed with his insecurities, his court, and his pathetic dreams of glory. They were all too busy, too concerned, too wrapped up in other things.

I've been asking myself the past few years whether I have also missed Christmas. Have I been too busy, too preoccupied with material concerns and what others might think if things are not just right? Am I in danger of missing the real meaning of Christmas? I don't think for a moment the Lord would have us dampen the excitement of Christmas. After all, He Himself has given us "all things to enjoy" (1 Timothy 6:17).

Perhaps this year our Christmas lists should include more attention to our toddlers, more time and appreciation for our parents and our mates, more unconditional acceptance of our teenagers, and more love and concern for our friends.

And what about our gift to the One whose birthday we celebrate? All He asks is the gift of ourselves—with all our faults and failures, problems and fears. This is Christmas: God giving, our receiving, God fulfilling.

Blessed Christmas!

—GIGI GRAHAM TCHIVIDJIA

HOLIDAY CRAFTING

Thread Angel

Use a piece of cardboard cut to the length of the angel you wish to make. Take white crochet thread and wrap it around the cardboard from top to bottom. The thickness of the angel will be determined by how many times you wrap the thread.

Carefully slide the thread off the cardboard and tie a string through the top part. Then cut the thread on the bottom. Turn the thread over so it will cover where you tied; measure down for a head and tie another piece to separate the head from the body.

For the wings, separate some of the thread; fold to shape a wing and tie. Tie it where the knot will be hidden on the back of the angel. After making the wings, starch the angel and iron her dress flat. After the angel dries, glue white eyelet lace to the bottom. Add a bow, flower, etc., to the front and perhaps tiny white pearl beads around the neck and for the halo.

—CHARLENE DICKERSON

CHAPTER TWO

Bring a Torch, Jeanette, Isabella

BRING A TORCH, JEANETTE, ISABELLA
(UN FLAMBEAU, JEANETTE, ISABELLA)

Bring a torch, Jeanette, Isabella,
Bring a torch to the stable run!
It is Jesus, good folks of the village;
Christ is born and Mary's calling:
Ah! ah! beautiful is the mother,
Ah! ah! beautiful is her son!

It is wrong when the child is sleeping,
It is wrong to talk so loud;
Silence, all, as you gather around,
Lest your noise should waken Jesus:
Hush! hush! see how fast he slumbers:
Hush! hush! see how fast he sleeps!

Softly to the little stable,
Softly for a moment come;
Look and see how charming is Jesus,
How he is white, his cheeks are rosy!
Hush! hush! see how the child is sleeping;
Hush! hush! see how he smiles in his dreams.

—TRADITIONAL SEVENTEENTH-CENTURY FRENCH CAROL FROM PROVENCE

The Santons of Provence

One of my very favorite Christmas cards showed the child Jesus standing in front of the sheepfold with open arms, welcoming people from all nations, cultures, and walks of life. The following story of the santons reminded me of this card.

—RUTH BELL GRAHAM

The santons of Provence are the heart of French Noel. The simplicity of these manger figures, the rural charm of their humble dress, their incredible variety are unique.

All the characters of the old French countryside are found among the santons, or little saints. Placed in the crèche, they resemble real people, in the detail of their expressions and in their clothes. There is the heavy garlic woman, with her warts and wrinkles, and the mayor in his tidy dress. The fisherwoman appears, her basket full of catches from the sea, and so do the gypsies in their colorful clothes and jewelry. A shepherd stands among the santons, a lamb in his arms. The shepherdess stands beside him, perhaps chatting with the village gossip.

Many of the santons are placed so that they are on their way to see Little Jesus in the manger. A drummer boy leads them, and a boy with a fife. Each santon has a gift to offer the Christ Child in His manger: a chicken, a basket of fruit, some flowers. The town simpleton is always the exception: he can only throw up his hands in amazement that the Son of God has come to earth. And the blind man, also present, has nothing to offer but a prayer.

The gifts from the santons are not so precious as those of the Three Kings, also represented at the crèche. But the presents of the folk are far more touching—simple gifts, given wholeheartedly by simple people.

No one is excluded: the baker, the pastry maker and the hunter, who turns aside his gun. Even unsavory characters—convicts, thieves, and pickpockets may take their place in the crèche, making it a true representation of society.

The history of the santons began in the early 1800s, when a group of Italian peddlers came to Marseille. The peddlers brought with them small, brightly painted figures made of clay, which they sold in the city's streets and markets.

Local artisans were so delighted with the little figures that they began to make santons, too, in French dress of the period. Artisans have been doing so ever since, and their work is considered some of the finest in the world.

The santons are a true regional art form. No matter how many versions of the crèche one may see in France today, the classic French manger scene is the one that includes the exquisite santons of Provence.

There are two types of santons: the santons d'argile, clay figures, and the santons habillés, clothed figures. The clothed are delightful, like dolls. But they take second place to the beloved clay santons.

Making santons is a family occupation in Provence, with everyone helping out in some way. Many santon makers are the product of several generations of artisans, from great-grandfather down. Creating the figures is a difficult, time-consuming art, taught by fathers and mothers to the youngsters, who assist after school and during vacations.

There are some first-generation santon makers, but the art is not easy to learn as an adult. Many of the "new" santon makers have married into families of santon artisans.

The clay figures are molded in two halves; when they are pressed together, the clay fuses into a whole. Then the artist creates exactly the appearance or expression he wants. Separate parts such as hats, baskets, and other accessories are attached to the body with a special adhesive.

As the figure dries and hardens, it gradually changes color. When completely dry, it is given a bath in a solution of gelatin to harden it further and to give it a special gloss. This covering provides a good surface for the application of coloring pigments. Without it, the colors would run.

Then the santons are lined up in rows, one type of character per row. All the millers will be together, for instance, or all the winemakers. Their faces are painted first, then the hair and the clothing and any accessories.

Until the end of the 1800s, clay santons were not fired in kilns, but merely dried in the sun. Even as late as 1945, many santon makers clung to the old open-air tradition. A few still do today. But the classic, old-style santons are so fragile that they tend to break, so most santon makers now usually fire them for longer life and durability.

Each year in Marseille, a special santon fair is held. It is an old fair, dating back to 1803. There are not many santon makers, and only a few dozen come to set up their displays in Les Alées, the market spot where the fair takes place.

Over a hundred different types of clay and clothed santons may be exhibited at one stand—a full year's work. Each santon maker has a separate stand, with the family on hand to help with the sales. All are proud of their work, and, if asked about their background, may reply, "Moi? Je suis né a la foire!" or "Me? I was born at the fair!"

The setting of the French crèche is seldom that of ancient Bethlehem. The santons are instead placed in the French countryside, where they belong. With them, there will be animals, too: the ox and the donkey are especially important. It is their breath that warms the Christ Child.

There are other animals of the farmlands: dogs, cats, pigs, horses, sheep, and lambs. Sometimes, the santon makers import animals from exotic areas. There may be camels, elephants, or a leopard or two mingling with the other figures.

Many magnificent antique crèches with their lovely santons are seen today in churches and in homes. Museums particularly treasure them and carefully preserve the crèches, bringing them out each year for all to admire.

The church at Beausset in Provence has a crèche more than a hundred years old. Its santons are reunited only at Christmastime. The rest of the year, the treasured figures are scattered among the different families of the village, who care for them with great affection.

Another marvelous manger scene is at the church of Saint-Antoine Ginestière, in Nice. The background is a miniature medieval castle, set on a mountaintop.

And, in Vaucluse, at La Crémade, there is a crèche to rival any of the others. The spectacular manger scene is rebuilt each year by devoted artisans. Every Christmas the crèche is given a different setting to represent one of the villages of Comtat Venaissin.

To be sure, there are crèches in France that differ from the traditional Provençal type. They appear made of wood, paper, and porcelain. Some have been composed of innovative materials such as sugar lumps and breadcrumbs. Knitted and crocheted figures take their place occasionally. There are even animated crèches, such as the one found in the tiny church atop a hill overlooking the old quarter of Cannes, on the Riviera. A series of weights and pulleys move its figures. As the images reenact the Nativity scene, a chorus of angels sings.

But, innovation aside, the French always go back to their favorite when thinking of the crèche as it should be: a place of simplicity, where everyone belongs. They think of the crèche of Provence. There, all the humble santons stand near the Christ Child, Who welcomes them all.

—FROM "CHRISTMAS IN FRANCE"
WORLD BOOK ENCYCLOPEDIA

CHRISTMAS IN PROVENCE

*F*or my father, who was faithful to ancient custom, the feast of the year was Christmas Eve. That day the farm laborers finished their work early, and off they would go with gifts from my mother wrapped in a napkin—a great galette l'buile, a roll of nougat, a cluster of dried figs, a sheep's milk cheese from our own sheep, a salad of celery and a bottle of matured wine. Off the peasants would go to "place the log" in their own homes. Those who stayed at the farm were those with no home to go to, or sometimes a relative, who was perhaps an old bachelor, would arrive at night saying, "Merry Christmas! I've come to place the log with all of you."

Then all together we would go joyously to find the Christmas log, which according to strict tradition, had to be from a fruit tree. We heaved it back to the farm, one after the other, with the eldest at one end and the youngest at the rear. Three times we would drag it around the kitchen, and when we arrived in front of the hearth, my father would pour a glass of mature wine solemnly over the log saying,

Happiness!
My fine children,
May God fill us all with happiness!
With Christmas comes all good things good!
May God grant that we see the next year through,
And even if there are not more of us, let there not be fewer!

And crying together, "Happiness, Happiness, Happiness," we placed the log on the hearth, and as the first flame licked from it, my father would cross himself and recite, "To the Log, at the heart of the fire!" Then we would all have supper.

—FREDRIC MISTRAL
FROM *CHRISTMAS AROUND THE WORLD*

A Southern Yule Log–Pumpkin Roll

Beat eggs for 5 minutes. Add sugar and pumpkin. Blend. Add flour and allspice. Blend. Spread in a prepared jelly roll pan and bake for 15 minutes at 375°.

Sprinkle a towel with powdered sugar. Turn pumpkin sheet cake onto the towel and roll up. Cool.

Pumpkin Roll

3 eggs

1 cup of sugar

2/3 cup solid packed pumpkin

3/4 cup plain flour

1 tablespoon allspice

powdered sugar

Filling

8 ounces cream cheese

1 cup powdered sugar

1/2 teaspoon vanilla

4 tablespoons butter

Mix filling ingredients until mixture reaches a frosting consistency. Roll pumpkin sheet cake back out into a flat cake. Frost the surface of the pumpkin cake and reroll in wax paper. Refrigerate, slice, and serve.

—JACKIE CAMBY AND ANN SLUDER

CHAPTER THREE

Down in Yon Forest

DOWN IN YON FOREST

Down in yon forest there stands a hall:
The bells of paradise I heard them ring;
It's covered all over with purple and pall:
And I love my Lord Jesus above anything.

Down under that bed there runs a flood,
The bells of paradise, I heard them ring,
The half it runs water, the half it runs blood,
And I love my Lord Jesus above anything.

Down at the bed feet there springs a thorn,
The bells of paradise, I heard them ring,
It bloomed its white blossoms the day He was born,
And I love my Lord Jesus above anything.

Over that place the moon shines bright,
The bells of paradise, I heard them ring,
To show that our Savior was born this night,
And I love my Lord Jesus above everything.

—TRADITIONAL ENGLISH CAROL

Why the Chimes Rang

There was once, in a far-away country where few people have ever traveled, a wonderful church. It stood on a high hill in the midst of a great city; and every Sunday, as well as on sacred days like Christmas, thousands of people climbed the hill to its great archways, looking like lines of ants all moving in the same direction.

When you came to the building itself, you found stone columns and dark passages, and a grand entrance leading to the main room of the church. This room was so long that one standing at the doorway could scarcely see to the other end, where the choir stood by the marble altar. In the farthest corner was the organ; and this organ was so loud, that sometimes when it played, the people for miles around would close their shutters and prepare for a great thunderstorm. Altogether, no such church as this was ever seen before, especially when it was lighted up for some festival, and crowded with people, young and old. But the strangest thing about the whole building was the wonderful chime of bells.

At one corner of the church was a great gray tower, with ivy growing over it as far up as one could see. I say as far as one could see, because the tower was quite great enough to fit the great church, and it rose so far into the sky that it was only in very fair weather that anyone claimed to be able to see the top. Even then one could not be certain that it was in sight. Up, and up, and up climbed the stones and the ivy; and, as the men who built the church had been dead for hundreds of years, every one had forgotten how high the tower was supposed to be.

Now all the people knew that at the top of the tower was a chime of Christmas bells. They had hung there ever since the church had been built, and were the most beautiful bells in the world. Some thought it was because a great musician had cast them and arranged them in their place; others said it was because of the great height, which reached up where the air was clearest and purest: however that might be, no one who had ever heard the chimes denied that they were the sweetest in the world. Some described them as sounding like angels far up in the sky; others, as sounding like strange winds singing through the trees.

But the fact was that no one had heard them for years and years. There was an old man living not far from the church, who said that his mother had spoken of hearing them when she was a little girl, and he was the only one who was sure of as much as that. They were Christmas chimes, you see, and were not meant to be played by men or on common days. It was the custom on Christmas Eve for all the people to bring to the church their offerings to the Christ-child; and when the greatest and best offering was laid on the altar, there used to come sounding through the music of the choir the Christmas chimes far up in the tower. Some said that the wind rang them, and others that they were so high that the angels could set them swinging. But for many long years they had never been heard. It was said that people had been growing less careful of their gifts for the Christ-child, and that no offering was brought great enough to deserve the music of the chimes.

Every Christmas Eve the rich people still crowded to the altar, each one trying to bring some better gift than any other, without giving anything that he wanted for himself, and the church was crowded with those who thought that perhaps the wonderful bells might be heard again. But although the service was splendid, and the offerings plenty, only the roar of the wind could be heard, far up in the stone tower.

Now, a number of miles from the city, in a little country village, where nothing could be seen of the great church but glimpses of the tower when the weather was fine, lived a boy named Pedro, and his little brother. They knew very little about the Christmas chimes, but they had heard of the service in the church on Christmas Eve, and had a secret plan, which they had often talked over when by themselves, to go to see the beautiful celebration.

"Nobody can guess, Little Brother," Pedro would say, "all the fine things there are to see and hear; and I have even heard it said that the Christ-child sometimes comes down to bless the service. What if we could see Him?"

The day before Christmas was bitterly cold, with a few lonely snowflakes flying in the air, and a hard white crust on the ground. Sure enough, Pedro and Little Brother were able to slip quietly away early in the afternoon; and although the walking was hard in the frosty air, before nightfall they had trudged so far, hand in hand, that they saw the lights of the big city just ahead of them. Indeed, they were about to enter one of the great gates in the wall that surrounded it, when they saw something dark on the snow near their path, and stepped aside to look at it.

It was a poor woman, who had fallen just outside the city, too sick and tired to get in where she might have found shelter. The soft snow made of a drift a sort of pillow for her, and she would soon be so sound asleep, in the wintry air, that no one could ever waken her again. All this Pedro saw in a moment, and he knelt down beside her and tried to rouse her, even tugging at her arm a little, as though he would have tried to carry her away. He turned her face toward him, so that he could rub some of the snow on it, and when he had looked at her silently a moment he stood up again and said:

"It's no use, Little Brother. You will have to go on alone."

"Alone?" cried Little Brother. "And you not see the Christmas festival?"

"No," said Pedro, and he could not keep back a bit of a choking sound in his throat. "See this poor woman. Her face looks like the Madonna in the chapel window, and she will freeze to death if nobody cares for her. Everyone has gone to the church now, but when you come back you can bring someone to help her. I will rub her to keep her from freezing, and perhaps get her to eat the bun that is left in my pocket."

"But I cannot bear to leave you, and go on alone," said Little Brother.

"Both of us need not miss the service," said Pedro, "and it had better be I than you. You can easily find your way to the church; and you must see and hear everything twice, Little Brother—once for you and once for me. I am sure the Christ-child must know how I should love to come with you and worship Him; and oh! if you get a chance, Little Brother, to slip up to the altar without getting in anyone's way, take this little silver piece of mine, and lay it down for my offering, when no one is looking. Do not forget where you have left me, and forgive me for not going with you."

In this way he hurried Little Brother off to the city, and winked hard to keep back the tears, as he heard the crunching footsteps sounding farther and farther away in the twilight. It was pretty hard to lose the music and splendor of the Christmas celebration that he had been planning for so long, and spend the time instead in that lonely place in the snow.

The great church was a wonderful place that night. Everyone said that it had never looked so bright and beautiful before. When the organ played and the thousands of people sang, the walls shook with the sound, and little Pedro, away outside the city wall, felt the earth tremble around him.

At the close of the service came the procession with the offerings to be laid on the altar. Rich men and great men marched proudly up to lay down their gifts to the Christ-child. Some brought wonderful jewels, some baskets of gold so heavy that they could scarcely carry them down the aisle. A great writer laid down a book that he had been making for years and years. And last of all walked the king of the country, hoping with all the rest to win for himself the chiming of the Christmas bells. There went a great murmur through the church, as the people saw the king take from his head the royal crown, all set with precious stones, and lay it gleaming on the altar, as his offering to the Holy Child. "Surely," everyone said, "we shall hear the bells now, for nothing like this has ever happened before."

But still only the cold old wind was heard in the tower, and the people shook their heads; and some of them said, as they had before, that they never really believed the story of the chimes, and doubted if they ever rang at all.

The procession was over, and the choir began the closing hymn. Suddenly the organist stopped playing (as though he had been shot) and everyone looked at the old minister who was standing by the altar, holding up his hand for silence. Not a sound could be heard from anyone in the church, but as all the people strained their ears to listen, there came softly, but distinctly, swinging through the air, the sound of the chimes in the tower. So far away, and yet so clear the music seemed. So much sweeter were the notes than anything that had been heard before, rising and falling away up there in the sky, that the people in the church sat for a moment as still as though something held each of them by the shoulders. Then they all stood up together and stared straight at the altar, to see what great gift had awakened the long-silent bells.

But all that the nearest of them saw was the childish figure of Little Brother, who had crept softly down the aisle when no one was looking, and had laid Pedro's little piece of silver on the altar.

—Raymond MacDonald Alden

HOLIDAY CRAFTING

Traditional Bell

The bell is a traditional tree orna-
ment, whose heritage goes back to the
sixth century when Christendom first
became fascinated with them. This most
traditional of all bells is the simplest of ornaments to make. It looks most spectacular when you
construct it out of silver, white and gold paper.

DIRECTIONS: Cut out several of the bell pieces from each color paper.
(See diagram for shape.) Fold them along the center line. Staple or glue the
many different bell pieces together at this center point. Attach a gold cord from the top
of the bell for hanging on the tree.

—FROM "CHRISTMAS IN GERMANY"
WORLD BOOK ENCYCLOPEDIA

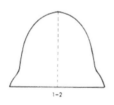

1–2

3–4

Links in the Chain of Memory

Tradition says that plum pudding is the symbol of Christmas. The round pudding represents the good and abundant earth. The holly berries stand for the blood of Christ. The flames of brandy are the flames of hell that are rapidly burned away as goodness triumphs over all. If plum pudding can mean all that—then let's raise our forks in celebration of life renewed.

Stir-up Sunday is the Sunday before Advent Sunday when the Church of England collect begins, "Stir up, we beseech Thee, O Lord, the wills of Thy faithful people: that they, plenteously bringing forth the fruit of good works . . ." Irreverent choirboys parodied this with:

> Stir up, we beseech Thee,
> The pudding in the pot.
> And when we do get home tonight
> We'll eat it up all hot.

The prayer is a reminder to stir up real as well as spiritual goodies, and this is traditionally the day on which the family gathers together to make the plum pudding. They have been doing this since the beginning of time, or if not the beginning, way back yonder in time. Not everyone understands it. In 1658 the Chevalier d'Arvieux described the plum pudding as "a detestable compound of scraped biscuits of flour, suet, currants, salt and pepper made into a paste, wrapped in a cloth, and boiled in a pot of broth."

Well, what did he know? He was a foreigner. Besides, whether you like it or not is wholly irrelevant. It is something you have to have. It is a kind of gastronomic patriotism, though it began humbly enough.

It started as a kind of porridge, a soft gruel or soup, at first made with plums but later with raisins and currants and spices, especially ginger. These were stirred into a broth made from beef or mutton and thickened with brown bread crumbs. It didn't evolve into the admirable pudding as we know it today until well into the late 1600s. It needed time to transform itself into the real thing, a noble pudding that would culminate the dinner with a flaming climax.

Some families still make their own plum pudding, remembering to stir it clockwise, as the earth moves on its axis, for this will bring good luck and another wish may be granted as the pudding is stirred. And more luck will come to the person who finds in the pudding a coin, a ring, or a charm. The notion is that a coin will bring a year of wealth, obviously a ring will be a wedding, and a silver thimble means a happy life, but one of a spinster.

—I R E N A C H A L M E R S
F R O M C H R I S T M A S M E M O R I E S W I T H R E C I P E S

Plum Pudding–A Classic!

Cream butter and sugar. Beat in eggs and vanilla; stir in carrots, apples, raisins, and nuts. Sift together flour, soda, and salt; stir into creamed mixture. Add crumbs and mix well. Spoon into well-oiled 1 1/2 - quart mold. Cover securely with mold lid or several thicknesses of waxed paper tied in place with string. Place mold on a rack in covered kettle of boiling water. (Water should come halfway up on the mold.) Steam for 3 hours. Unmold pudding onto serving plate; flame if you wish (directions follow). Serve hot with warm Caramel Sauce. Makes 8 to 10 servings

CARAMEL SAUCE: Combine 1/2 cup brown sugar, firmly packed, I tablespoon cornstarch and 1/2 teaspoon salt in small saucepan. Add 1 cup boiling water; cook until thickened and clear, stirring constantly. Remove from heat and stir in 2 tablespoons **butter and 1 teaspoon vanilla.**

1/2 cup butter
1 1/2 cup brown sugar, firmly packed
2 eggs
1 teaspoon vanilla
1 cup grated peeled carrots
1 cup grated peeled apples
1/2 cup raisins
1 cup pecans, coarsely chopped
1 cup sifted flour
1 teaspoon baking soda
1/2 teaspoon salt
1 cup fine dry, white bread crumbs
Caramel Sauce

TO FLAME PUDDING: Soak sugar cubes in lemon extract tinted with red food coloring. Just before serving, place 2 or 3 cubes on top of pudding or several around sides, not touching pudding (use a metal or flame-proof dish). Light the cubes.

*I*n a household where there are five or six children, the eldest not above ten or eleven, the making of the pudding is indeed an event. It is thought of days, if not weeks, before. To be allowed to share in the noble work, is a prize for young ambition. . . . Lo! the lid is raised, curiosity stands on tip-toe, eyes sparkle with anticipation, little hands are clapped in ecstasy, almost too great to find expression in words. The hour arrives—the moment wished and feared; wished, oh! how intensely; feared, not in the event, but lest envious fate should not allow it to be an event, and mar the glorious concoction in its very birth.

And then when it is dished, when all fears of this kind are over, when the roast beef has been removed, when the pudding, in all the glory of its own splendor, shines upon the table, how eager is the anticipation of the near delight! How beautifully it steams! How delicious it smells! How round it is! A kiss is round, the horizon is round, the earth is round, the moon is round, the sun and stars, and all the host of heaven are round. So is plum pudding.

—FROM *ILLUSTRATED LONDON NEWS*
DECEMBER 1848

The pudding must be unusually huge, and darkly, deeply,

lugubriously blue in color. It must be stuck so full of plums

that the pudding itself will ooze out into the pan and not be

brought on to the table at all. I expect to be there by the twentieth,

to manage these little things myself,—remembering it is the

early Bird that catches the worm,—but give you the instructions

in case I should be delayed.

—KATE DOUGLAS WIGGIN
FROM *THE BIRDS' CHRISTMAS CAROL*

A QUIET KNOWING CHRISTMAS

CHAPTER FOUR

The Sussex Carol

SUSSEX CAROL

On Christmas night all Christians sing,
To hear the news the angels bring,
On Christmas night all Christians sing,
To hear the news the angels bring;
News of great joy, news of great mirth,
News of our merciful King's birth.

Then why should men on earth be sad,
Since our Redeemer made us glad,
Then why should men on earth be sad,
Since our Redeemer made us glad?
When from our sin he set us free,
All for to gain our liberty?

When sin departs before his grace,
Then life and health come in its place,
When sin departs before his grace,
Then life and health come in its place,
Angels and men with joy may sing,
All for to see the newborn King.

All out of darkness we have light,
Which made the angels sign this night,
All out of darkness we have light,
Which made the angels sign this night,
Glory to God and peace to men, Now and for evermore. Amen.

—TRADITIONAL ENGLISH CAROL

DAY BEFORE CHRISTMAS

We have been helping with the cake
And licking out the pan,
And wrapping up our packages
As neatly as we can.
And we have hung our stockings up
Beside the open grate,
And now there's nothing more to do
Except To Wait!

—MARCHETTE CHUTE

The True Story of Santa Claus

Some people have a problem with Santa Claus. In our family, however, we were always able to differentiate between Santa and the Christ Child and know who was more important.

On Christmas Eve, Bill would gather the children, and later the grandchildren, to place the annual call to Santa. "Santa," he would say into the phone, "This is Billy Graham from North Carolina, and I've got some excited children waiting for your arrival tonight." I even went so far as to make the children think Santa was arriving by ringing donkey bells in the chimney and leaving a strand of his beard on a nail or a boot print in the ashes.

I remember seeing a Christmas card once with Santa kneeling beside the manger. The following story helps us to understand the origin of Santa in the person of Saint Nicholas, and how the generosity of Saint Nick poured out from his love of Christ.

—RUTH BELL GRAHAM

If we should wake on the sixth of December and find our stockings full of candy and toys we should think that the ruddy old fellow who comes down the chimney had lost his wits and arrived about three weeks too soon. But his arrival would seem exactly on time to children in other parts of the world. For the feast of St.

Nicholas is the sixth of December, and how he became the patron saint of the day of the Saint of saints, the Christ child, is a story. . . .

Nicholas was an actual person. Though he is the most popular saint in the calendar, not excepting St. Christopher and St. Francis, we know little about the man to whom so many lovely deeds, human and miraculous, have been ascribed. He was bishop of Myra, in Lycia, Asia Minor, in the first part of the fourth century of the Christian Era. Asia Minor is far away from reindeer and Santy Claus, but the world of faith and fable is small and ideas travel far if they have centuries of time for their journey round the world. And Asia Minor is the cradle of all Christian ideas. From the day of his birth Nicholas revealed his piety and grace. He refused on fast days to take the natural nourishment of a child. He was the youngest bishop in the history of the church. He was persecuted and imprisoned with many other Christians during the reign of the Roman emperor Diocletian, and was released and honored when Constantine the Great established the Christian Church as the official religion, or at least recognized and encouraged it. Under Constantine, in 325, was held the first general council of the Christians at Nicaea, where many important matters were decided. These matters belong to theology and are not in our picture, but Nicholas may have had a hand, a vigorous hand, in them. One of the arguers who seemed to Nicholas, and to the later orthodox church, a dangerous heretic, so roused the righteous ire of the saint that Nicholas smote him in the jaw. . . .

About two hundred years after his death Nicholas was a great figure in Christian legend, and Justinian, the last powerful Roman emperor in the East, built a church in honor of St. Nicholas in Constantinople. But the bones of the saint were not allowed to rest in peace in his hometown, Myra, where he was probably buried. About seven hundred years after his death, in the eleventh century, what remained of the earthly Nicholas was dug up and moved to the city of Bari, in Italy. In its day it was one of many important seaports that dominated Mediterranean traffic. The merchants of Bari organized a predatory expedition to the burial place of Nicholas, stole the bones, reburied them in Bari and built a church, which was long an objective for religious pilgrims and is still worth the travel of a lover of art and architecture. The city of Venice, not to be outdone by a rival maritime town, also claims to enshrine the bones of the saint. So the curious tourist may take his choice. The bones are dust, wherever they lie. The churches in Bari and in many cities of Europe still stand; there are more than four hundred dedicated to Nicholas in England. More important, the spirit of the saint is alive throughout the Christian world.

Nicholas was not a barefoot recluse vowed to poverty. His father was a wealthy merchant, and his riches, inherited or created by the magic wand which fairy godfathers wield, enabled him to be a dispenser of the good things of life, an earthly representative of the Supreme Giver of gifts.

The most famous episode in his long career of benevolence is his rescue of the three dowerless maidens. An impoverished nobleman had three daughters whom he was about to send forth into a life of shame. Nicholas heard of the tragic situation and at night threw a purse of gold into the house. This furnished the dowry for the eldest daughter, and she was married.

After a little while, says the Golden Legend, which is the great medieval story of the saints, this holy hermit of God "threw in another mass of gold" and that provided a dowry for the second daughter. "And after a few days Nicholas doubled the mass of gold and cast it into the house." So the third daughter was endowed. The happy father, wishing to know his benefactor, ran after Nicholas and recognized him, but the holy man "required him not to tell nor discover this thing as long as he lived."

Thus Nicholas became not only the generous giver but the special patron saint of maidenhood and was so known and celebrated throughout the Middle Ages. Dante speaks in three short lines, as if he assumed that everybody already knew the story, of the generosity of Nicholas to maidens, "to lead their youth to honor." The Italian painters made much of this story. A fine pictorial representation of it is in the Metropolitan Art Museum in New York City. It is one of those dramatic paintings in which the old artists told a really moving tale long before the days of the camera and the moving picture. Inside the house you see the three distressed daughters and the still more dejected and ragged father. Outside is Nicholas climbing up at the door in the act of throwing the purse through a little window.

The story takes what seems an almost humorous turn. Let us imagine three purses or "masses" of gold. We recognize them, in conventional form, in the three gold balls over the pawnbroker's shop.

Nicholas is honored and accepted with a kind of childish ignorance. Professor George H. McKnight of Ohio State University, who has given us the best account in English of the good St. Nicholas, begins his book by saying that strangely little is known of him in America. But he belongs to us by a very special inheritance. Our Dutch ancestors in New York—ancestry is a matter of tradition, not of blood—brought St. Nicholas over to New Amsterdam. The English colonists borrowed him from their Dutch neighbors. The Dutch form is San Nicolaas. If we say that rather fast with a stress on the broad double-*A* of the last syllable, a *D* or a *T* slips in after the *N* and we get "Sandyclaus" or "Santy Claus." And our American children are probably the only ones in the world who say it just that way; indeed the learned, and very British, *Encyclopaedia Britannica* calls our familiar form "an American corruption" of the Dutch. I suspect, however, that we should hear something very like it from the lips of children in Holland and Germany; in parts of southern Germany the word in sound, and I think in spelling, is "Santiklos."

However that may be, America owes the cheery saint of Christmas to Holland and

Germany. In Belgium and Holland the festival of the saint is still observed on his birthday, December sixth, and the jollities and excitements are much the same as those that we enjoy at Christmas, with some charming local variations. St. Nicholas is not the merry fellow with a chubby face and twinkling eye, but retains the gravity appropriate to a venerable bishop. He rides a horse or a donkey instead of driving a team of reindeer. He leaves his gifts in stockings, shoes or baskets. And for children who have been very naughty, and whose parents cannot give him a good account of them, he leaves a rod by way of admonition, for he is a highly moral saint, though kind and forgiving. If the parents are too poor to buy gifts, the children say ruefully that the saint's horse has glass legs and has fallen down and broken his foot. The horse or donkey of St. Nicholas is not forgotten; the children leave a wisp of hay for him, and in the morning it is gone.

As with us, the older people have their own festivities, suppers, exchange of gifts, surprises. But also as with our Christmas, the feast of Nicholas is primarily a day for children. . . .

As the Christian faith grew, the Church encouraged all the popular customs, or many of them, took them over and associated them with Christian holidays. This may have been a deliberate attempt of the priests to win the favor of the people and make the new religion popular, or the people may have made the transfer themselves by the vague and untraceable but very real process of folk poetry. . . .

No other saint and few other men embrace such a wide variety of benevolent ideas as Nicholas, with such duration in time and such extent throughout the Christian world. And he is probably the only serious figure in religious history in any way associated with humor, with the spirit of fun. For he is the patron of giving. And it is fun to give.

—JOHN MACY

Is There a Santa Claus?

6 P.M., DECEMBER 23

I am writing this on the plane from New York to Los Angeles. We are in bad
weather. The plane bumps up and down. The visibility is zero. The passengers
are nervous; almost every one of them is going home for Christmas. Most of them have
to connect in Los Angeles with other flights. That includes me. My flight to Honolulu
and home departs at 10 P.M.

But I have another problem. When I get home to Honolulu tomorrow, I must have
a Christmas story ready to tell the neighborhood children. They have asked me to title
it, "How do I know there's a Santa Claus?" I believe they're pulling my leg. The youngsters are seven to sixteen years old. They're smart and skeptical.

8:10 P.M.

The pilot has just given us bad news. Los Angeles is fogged in; no aircraft can land.
We have to detour to Ontario, California, an emergency field not far from Los Angeles.

3:12 A.M., DECEMBER 24

The sun hasn't risen yet. It's dark, damp, and chilly. What with one problem and
another, we have just landed in Ontario, California—six hours behind schedule.
Everyone is cold, exhausted, hungry, and irritable. All of us on the plane will miss our

connections. Many will not make it home tonight in time for Christmas Eve. I am in no mood to make up a story about Santa Claus even though I had promised the children.

I wonder when we'll get out of this emergency field at Ontario. What a mess! Santa Claus? Bah! Humbug!

7:15 A.M., DECEMBER 24

I am writing this at the Los Angeles airport, having just arrived here by bus from Ontario.

A lot has happened in the last four hours. The airfield at Ontario, where we made an emergency landing about 3 A.M. was bedlam. Many Los Angeles–bound planes had to land there. The frantic passengers—it seems like several thousand of them—had hoped to get word to their families that they would be late and might not make it home for Christmas Eve. But the telegraph office was closed, and there were endless lines at the three telephone booths. No food. No coffee.

The employees at the small terminal were just as frenzied and fatigued as the passengers. Everything had gone wrong. Baggage was heaped helter-skelter, regardless of destination. No one knew which buses would go where, or at what time. Babies were crying, women were shouting questions, men were bellowing commands to which no one paid attention. In the effort to find luggage, the mob swarmed and jostled like an army of frightened ants. People shoved each other, swore, and complained. The loudspeakers crackled and blared announcements, which were difficult to understand.

It hardly seemed possible that this was the day of Christmas Eve.

Suddenly, amid the nervous commotion, I heard a confident, unhurried voice. It stood out like a great church bell—clear, calm, and filled with love.

"Now don't you worry, ma'am," the voice said. "We're going to find your luggage and get you to La Jolla in time. Everything's going to be just fine."

This was the first positive, constructive statement I had heard since landing.

I turned and saw a man who might have stepped right out of "The Night before Christmas." He was short and stout, with a florid, merry face. On his head was some sort of official cap, the kind that sightseeing guides wear. Tumbling out beneath were cascades of curly white hair. He wore hiking boots, as if, perhaps, he had just arrived after a snowy trip behind a team of reindeer. Pulled snugly over his barrel chest and fat tummy was a red sweatshirt.

The man stood next to a homemade pushcart, composed of an enormous packing box resting on four bicycle wheels. It contained urns of steaming coffee and piles of miscellaneous cardboard cartons.

"Here you are, ma'am," said the roly-poly man with the red sweatshirt and the cheerful voice. "Have some hot coffee while we look for your luggage."

Pushing the cart before him, pausing only long enough to hand coffee to others, or to say a cheerful "Merry Christmas to you, brother!" or to promise that he would be back to help, he searched among the sprawling piles of luggage. Finally he found the woman's possessions. Placing them on the pushcart, he said to her, "You just follow me. We'll put you on the bus to La Jolla."

After getting her settled, Kris Kringle (that's what I had started calling him) returned to the terminal. I found myself tagging along and helping him with the coffee. I knew that my bus wouldn't leave for a while yet.

Kris Kringle stood out like a beam of light in that murky, noisy, dismal field. There was something about him that made everyone smile. Dispensing coffee, blowing a child's nose, laughing, singing snatches of Christmas songs, he calmed panicky passengers and sped them on their way.

When a woman fainted, it was Kris Kringle who

pushed through the helpless group around her. From one of his cartons he produced smelling salts and a blanket. When the woman was conscious again, he asked three men to carry her into the terminal building and told them to use the loudspeaker system to find a doctor.

I wondered, *Who is this funny, stout little man who gets things done?*

I asked him, "What company do you work for?"

"Sonny," he said to me, "see that kid over there in the blue coat? She's lost. Give her this candy bar, and tell her to stay right where she is. If she wanders around, her mother won't ever find her."

I did as ordered, then repeated, "What company do you work for?"

"Shucks, I'm not working for anyone. I'm just having fun. Every December I spend my two weeks' vacation helping travelers. What with this rush season there is always somebody who needs a hand. Hey, look what we have over here."

He had spotted a tearful young mother with a baby. Winking at me, Kris Kringle perked his cap at a jaunty angle and rolled his cart over to them. The woman was sitting on her suitcase, clutching her child.

"Well, well, sister," he said, "that's a mighty pretty baby you have. What's the trouble?"

Between sobs, the young woman told him that she hadn't seen her husband for over a year. She was to meet him at a hotel in San Diego. He wouldn't know what had delayed her, and would worry. And the baby was hungry.

From the pushcart Kris Kringle took a bottle of warmed milk. "Now don't you worry. Everything will be all right."

As he guided her to the bus for Los Angeles—the one I was to leave on—he wrote in his notebook her name and the name of the hotel in San Diego. He helped her onto the bus and promised her that he would get a message to her husband.

"God bless you," she said, making herself comfortable and cradling the now sleeping child in her arms. "I hope you have a merry Christmas and many wonderful presents."

"Thank you, sister," he said, tipping his cap. "I've already received the greatest gift of all, and you gave it to me—Oh, oh," he said, looking out the bus window. "There's an old fellow in trouble. Good-bye, sister. I'm going over there and give myself another present."

He got off the bus. I got off, too, since the bus wouldn't leave for a few minutes. He turned to me.

"Say," he said, "aren't you taking this jalopy to Los Angeles?"

"Yes."

"Okay, you've been a good assistant. Now I want to give you a Christmas present. You sit next to that lady and look after her and the baby. When you get to Los Angeles"—he tore a piece of paper from his notebook—"telephone her husband at this hotel in San Diego. Tell him about his family's delay."

He knew what my answer would be, because he left without even waiting for a reply. I sat down next to the young mother, took the baby from her. Looking out the window, I saw Kris Kringle in his bulging red sweatshirt disappearing into the crowd.

The bus started. I felt good. I began thinking of home and Christmas. And I knew then how I would answer the question of the children in my neighborhood: "How do I know there's a Santa Claus?"

How do I know there's a Santa Claus? Gracious, friends, I've met him!

—WILLIAM J. LEDERER
FROM *A HAPPY BOOK OF HAPPY STORIES*

CHAPTER FIVE

Lo, How a Rose E'er Blooming

LO, HOW A ROSE E'ER BLOOMING

Lo, how a Rose e'er blooming
From tender stem hath sprung!
Of Jesse's lineage coming
As men of old have sung.
It came, a flow'ret bright,
Amid the cold of winter,
When half spent was the night.

Isaiah 'twas foretold it,
The Rose I have in mind,
With Mary we behold it,
The Virgin Mother kind.
To show God's love aright,
She bore to men a Savior,
When half spent was the night.

O flower, whose fragrance tender
With sweetness fills the air,
Dispel in glorious splendor
The darkness everywhere;
True man, yet very God,
From sin and death now save us,
And share our every load.

—FOURTEENTH-CENTURY GERMAN MELODY
VERSES 1 AND 2, ORIGINAL TEXT, SIXTEENTH-CENTURY GERMAN
VERSE 3, NINETEENTH-CENTURY GERMAN

The Story of "Lo, How a Rose E'er Blooming"

Christmas is a time of miracles. The angelic chorus, lowly shepherds (the first recipients of the heavenly announcement), a humble manger as the birthplace of deity—all are miraculous happenings. And the amazing wonder is that all of these events were foretold centuries before they occurred. From Genesis to Malachi, the Old Testament writers point to the coming of a Messiah, one who would reestablish a "son" relationship with the human race.

The prophet Isaiah is called the messianic prophet, he being the one who "saw [Jesus'] glory and spoke of Him" (John 12:41 NKJV). Seven centuries before our Lord's birth, Isaiah wrote of Christ's deity, His earthly ministry, His death, and His eternal reign. He described Christ's advent into the world: "And there shall come forth a rod out of the stem of Jesse, and a Branch shall grow out of his roots: And the spirit of the LORD shall rest upon him" (Isaiah 11:1–2).

"Lo! How a Rose E'er Blooming" is based on these Old Testament prophecies concerning the "rose of Sharon," an epithet for Christ (Song of Solomon 2:1). The German carol is thought to have come from the fifteenth century, when songs extolling the Virgin Mary (Warlenlieder) were especially popular (note this reference in verse two). As Protestants began making more use of this song, the focus became more on Jesus than on Mary. As is true of most of our ancient carols and folk music, the authorship of this German text is unknown.

Theodore Baker, a German-born scholar and translator of the first two verses, was the literary editor for the G. Schirmer Company in New York from 1892–1926. Harriet

Spaeth, translator of the third verse, was a Lutheran musician in Baltimore, Maryland. She edited the Lutheran Church Music Book in 1872.

There is an interesting expression used in the first two verses: "When half spent was the night." This no doubt refers to the long wait in human history for the "fullness of God's time" to happen. When it finally occurred, relatively few noticed. The third verse teaches a most important truth concerning our Savior's birth: Christ was "True man, yet very God."

—Kenneth W. Osbeck
from Joy to the World:
The Stories Behind Your Favorite Christmas Carols

The Christmas Rose

Of all Christmas decorations in France, the most important are flowers. No French housewife considers her holiday table complete without a lavish arrangement of some kind. Guests bring flowers, too, as a gesture of thanks to their hostess. Roses, gladioli, carnations, and snapdragons are favorite Christmas choices, along with a wide variety of dried flowers. Potted plants are also popular: red and white poinsettias, sweet-smelling hyacinths, multicolored azaleas, and Christmas begonias.

In some parts of France a very special flower graces the Christmas table. It is called the hellebore—a tiny blossom with creamy white petals, glossy leaves, and a dark green stem. The French call it the Christmas rose.

There's a lovely old legend about how this flower came to be, and how it got its special name. The story tells about a young bellringer named Nicaise, who lived in a village near Rouen. Nicaise was dull witted.

His guardian, a poor parish priest named Father Anthime, frequently scolded him for his foolishness. Once on Christmas Eve, after an especially severe scolding, Nicaise sadly went up into the church tower until it was time to ring the bells for the midnight Mass. He soon fell fast asleep.

The church tower was ornamented with several ugly gargoyles, stone rainspouts carved to look like horrible beasts with their tongues sticking out. As Nicaise slept, he dreamed one of the gargoyles came to life.

The gargoyle spoke to him, saying that it was actually the Devil. The gargoyle told Nicaise that it liked him, which pleased the boy. Nicaise was not terribly bright, please remember.

Then the gargoyle offered Nicaise three wishes. Nicaise thought a bit. Finally, he said: "I'd like to be smart, that's one. And rich, that's two. And married to a beautiful lady. That's three." The gargoyle agreed. Then Nicaise remembered that it was Christmas, and there were no flowers to decorate Father Anthime's little church.

"Please," he begged. "I also want some flowers for Father Anthime to place at the altar tonight."

The gargoyle spat with rage. That was too much. It told Nicaise to make do with what he already had been given. And the gargoyle added that it expected a little something in return. It demanded Nicaise's soul, in fact.

The gargoyle told the boy that it would return in exactly one year's time to take him away. "Unless," it laughed nastily, "unless on Christmas Eve one year from now, you can make flowers bloom in the snow!"

Nicaise woke up. What a strange dream, he thought. But was it really a dream? For as the months went by, all three wishes came true.

The full year passed, and it was once again Christmas Eve. Nicaise knew the Devil was coming for him that night. Frightened, he confessed his sins to Father Anthime.

The priest was horrified. "You've sold your soul," he cried, "and the Devil's coming to get you this very night— unless, by some miracle, you can actually make flowers bloom in the snow outside. My son, pray. Pray to the Good Lord, the angels, the saints, and to our Lord Jesus!"

The two knelt and prayed together as the midnight hour approached. Finally, thinking that the end was near, Nicaise crept sadly up the stairs to ring the bells one last time.

Just as he started to reach for the bell rope, he heard a cry from down below. Some children had wandered into the small church garden and they had found, of all things, flowers in the snow! Father Anthime came running, and when he saw the flowers, he began to weep.

"Nicaise," he called. "Come down, you are saved! We have won against the Devil. The Christ Child has sent flowers, real flowers—Christmas roses—to bloom in the snow!"

—from "Christmas in France"
World Book Encyclopedia

CHRISTMAS EVE

The door is on the latch tonight,
　　The hearth-fire is aglow,
I seem to hear soft passing feet
The Christ child in the snow.

My heart is open wide tonight
　　For stranger, kith or kin.
I would not bar a single door
Where Love might enter in.

—KATE DOUGLAS WIGGIN

*A*t Christmas season, we children became fascinated with snow. We saw pictures of Santa at the North Pole, flying through the sky behind his reindeer with white flakes swirling around the sleigh loaded with gifts. The Katzenjammer Kids and other characters in the funny papers were always building snowmen and having snowball battles. We actually saw a scattering of snowflakes a few times during our early years, and the first excited cries of "It's snowing! It's snowing!" would instantly empty our house or the classrooms. In my grandmother's house there was a small, clear globe filled with liquid that, if shaken, would cause white flakes to swirl around for a few moments. This helped us imagine how real snow would be.

—JIMMY CARTER
FROM *CHRISTMAS IN PLAINS: MEMORIES*

A QUIET KNOWING CHRISTMAS

Treasures of the Snow

Patricia St. John is one of my favorite authors. I'm not sure where I first became aware of her writing; perhaps it was from John Stott, a well-known preacher in England. The following is an excerpt from her delightful book Treasures of the Snow.

—RUTH BELL GRAHAM

It was Christmas Eve and Dani was five years old. It was a great day, because for the first time in his life he had been considered old enough to go down to the church with his eleven-year-old sister, Annette, to see the tree.

Now he sat up in bed, drinking a bowl of potato soup, his yellow head only just showing above his enormous white feather eiderdown, which was almost as far as it was broad. Annette sat beside him, and in her hand she held a shining gingerbread bear.

"I am sorry, Dani," she announced firmly, "but you cannot have it in the bed with you. It would be all crumbs by the morning. Look! I will put him here on the cupboard and the moon will shine in on him and you will be able to see him."

Dani opened his mouth to argue, but changed his mind, and filled his mouth with potato soup. It was unreasonable of his sister to object to his hugging his bear all night, but, after all, there were lots of other things to be happy about. Dani was always happy

60

from the moment he opened his eyes in the morning to the moment he closed them at night. Tonight he was happy because he had heard and seen the glittering tree, and been out in the snow by starlight. He handed his empty bowl to Annette and cuddled down under his feather-bed duvet.

"Do you think," he asked confidentially, "that Father Christmas would come if I put my slippers on the windowsill?" Annette looked rather startled, and wondered where he had heard of such a thing, for in Switzerland Father Christmas is not such a well-known person as he is in England. Swiss children have their Christmas bear from the tree on Christmas Eve, and presents from their family on New Year's Day. On Christmas Day they go to church and have a feast, and children get a present.

"They said," went on Dani, "that he came on a sleigh drawn by reindeer, and left presents in good children's slippers. Am I a good child, Annette?"

"Yes," answered Annette, kissing him. "You are a very good child, but you will not get a present from Father Christmas. He only goes to rich little boys."

Aren't I a rich little boy?" asked Dani, who thought life left nothing to be desired.

"No," replied Annette firmly, "you are not. We are poor and Papa has to work hard and Grandmother and I have to go on and on patching your clothes because we cannot afford to buy new ones."

Dani chuckled. "I don't mind being poor," he announced stoutly; "I like it. Now tell me a story, Annette; tell me about Christmas and the little Baby and the cows and the great big shining star."

So Annette told the story, and Dani, who should have been asleep, listened wide-eyed.

"I should have liked sleeping in the hay better than in the inn," he said when she had finished. "I should like to sleep with our cow, Paquerette; I think it would be fun."

Annette shook her head. "No, you wouldn't," she replied; "not in the winter, without a duvet; you would be very cold and unhappy and long for a warm bed. It was cruel of them to say there was no room for a little new baby; they could have made room somehow." The cuckoo clock on the stairs struck nine.

Annette jumped up.

"You must go to sleep, Dani," she said, "and I must make Papa's chocolate."

She kissed him, tucked him up, put out the light and left him; but Dani did not go to sleep. Instead, he lay staring out into the darkness, thinking hard.

He was not a greedy little boy, but he could not help thinking that if Father Christmas happened to come to their house it would be a great pity not to be ready. Of course, it was unlikely he would come, since Dani was only a poor child, but on the other hand it was just possible that he might. And, after all, it could do no harm to put out the little slipper even if there were nothing in it in the morning. The question was where to put it. He could not put it on the windowsill, because he could not open the high barred shutters by himself. Nor could he put it outside the front door, because the family was all sitting in the front room. The only place was just outside the back door on the little strip of snow that divided the kitchen from the hay barn. Of course, Father Christmas was very unlikely to see it there, but still, there was no harm in trying.

Dani's mind was made up. He crept out of bed and tiptoed cautiously across the bedroom and down the stairs. He went barefoot, because he did not want anyone to hear him, and in his hand he carried one small scarlet slipper, lined with rabbit fur. His father had shot the rabbit, and Annette had made the slippers, and Dani felt it might catch the eye of Father Christmas, as being something rather unusual in the way of slippers. It was a struggle to lift the great wooden bar that latched the kitchen door, and Dani had to stand on a stool before he managed it. He had a moment's bright vision of snow and starlight, and then the bitter air struck him like a knife, and almost took his breath away. He thrust the slipper on to the step, and shut the door again as quickly as he could.

Back to bed scuttled Dani with a light heart. He cuddled down under the clothes, curled himself into a ball and buried his nose in the pillows. He had already said his proper prayers with Annette before he got into bed, but now he had a little bit to add.

"Please, dear God," he whispered, "make Father Christmas and his reindeer come this way; and make him see my red slipper, and make him put a little present inside even if I am only a poor little boy."

And then the hump that was Dani rolled over sideways and fell asleep to dream, like thousands of other children the world over, of the old Gentleman in the red cloak careening over the snow to the jangle of reindeer bells.

He woke very early, because children always wake early on Christmas morning, and of course the first thing he thought of was the scarlet slipper. It was such an exciting thought that his heart beat quite thumpily, and he peeped over the top of his duvet to see whether Annette were awake.

But Annette was fast asleep, with her long fair hair spread all over the pillow, and for all Dani knew it might still have been the middle of the night. In fact, he had almost decided that it must still be the middle of the night, when he heard his father clattering the milk churns in the kitchen below.

So it must be Christmas morning, and Dani must get down quickly or his father would open the door and find his present before he did; for somehow Dani was absolutely sure that there would be a present. All his doubts of the night before had vanished in his sleep.

He crept out of the room without waking Annette, and slipped into the kitchen where his father was scalding the churns. His father did not see him until he felt two arms clasping his legs, and looked down; there was his son, rosy, bright-eyed and tousled, looking up at him.

"Has Father Christmas been?" asked Dani. Surely his father, who stayed up so late, and got up so early, must have heard the bells and the crunch of hoofs in the snow.

"Father Christmas?" repeated his father in bewilderment. "Why, no; he didn't come here. We live too far up the mountain for him."

But Dani shook his head. "We don't," he said eagerly. "His reindeers can go any- where, and I expect you were asleep and didn't hear him. Open the door for me, Papa dear, just in case he has left me a present."

His father wished he had known of this earlier, so that he could have put a chocolate stick on the step, for he hated to disappoint his boy. However, open the back door he must, to roll the churns across to the stable; so he lifted the latch, and in an instant Dani had dived between his legs like an eager rabbit, and was kneeling by his slipper in the snow.

Then he gave a wild, high-pitched scream of excitement and dived back again into the kitchen with his slipper in his arms.

A miracle had happened: Father Christmas had been and had left a present. And in all his happy five years of life, Dani had never seen such a perfect present before.

For curled up in the furry lining of his scarlet slipper was a tiny white kitten, with blue eyes and one black smudge on her nose. It was a weak, thin little kitten very nearly dead with cold and hunger, and had it not been for the warmth of the rabbit's fur it would certainly have been quite dead. But it still breathed lightly, and Dani's father, for- getting all about the churns, knelt down on the kitchen floor beside his son and set about restoring it.

First he wrapped it in a piece of hot flannel and laid it against the hot wall of the stove; then they heated milk in a pan and fed it with a spoon, as it was far too weak to suck. At first it only spluttered and dribbled, but after a while it put out a wee pink tongue and its dim blue eyes grew bright and interested. Then, after about five minutes or so, it twitched its tail and stretched itself. Finally, having had quite enough to eat, it curled itself back into a ball and set up a faint, contented purr.

All this time Dani and his father had not spoken one word, because they were so intent on what they were doing. But, now that their work was successfully finished for the time being, they sat back and looked at each other. Dani's cheeks were the color of poppies and his eyes shone like stars.

"I knew he would come," he whispered, "but I never guessed he would bring such a beautiful present; it is the most beautiful present I have ever had in all my life. What shall I call it, Papa?"

"You had better call it after the Christmas saint," said Papa; and he looked curiously at Dani with a sort of new respect. It certainly seemed a miracle.

He left the sleeping kitten in Dani's care and went to the stables. Sitting in the dim light with his head pressed against the flanks of the cows and the milk frothing into the pails, he tried to think of some explanation. Of course, the kitten had strayed across from the barn, but it did seem wonderful that it should  have found Dani's slipper and had been there all ready for him. After a while Dani's father decided that perhaps it was not so wonderful after all. Surely it was natural on Christmas night that the Father in Heaven, thinking of His own Son, should have been unwilling to disappoint a motherless child on earth.

Surely He guided the steps of the white kitten for the sake of the Babe born in Bethlehem. Dani's father paused for a moment in his milking and thanked God on behalf of his little son.

Annette appeared in the kitchen shortly afterwards to get breakfast, and stood still in amazement at the sight of Dani in his nightshirt and overcoat watching over a white kitten. She was about to ask questions when Dani put his finger on his lip and motioned her to be quiet, for he was very much afraid of waking the kitten. Then he tiptoed over to her, pulled her down on a chair, climbed on to her knee and whispered the whole strange story into her ear.

Annette had no difficulty in explaining it to herself. Being eleven years old she did not believe in Father Christmas, but she did believe in Christmas angels, and surely such a pure white kitten must have dropped straight from heaven. She sat down on the floor and gathered Dani and the kitten onto her lap; and here Grandmother found them half an hour later when she came in expecting to find her Christmas coffee steaming on the table.

—PATRICIA M. ST. JOHN
FROM *TREASURES OF THE SNOW*

Tissue Paper Roses

MATERIALS: tissue paper, red or white; florist's wire; green florist's tape; scissors; ruler; pencil

DIRECTIONS: Cut one 3-inch and one 4-inch square of tissue paper. Crumple 3-inch square into a ball; place ball at one corner of 4-inch square. Fold opposite corner of 4-inch square toward ball, sandwiching ball between layers of tissue and forming a triangle. Next, fold other two corners of triangle toward ball, then roll and twist folded paper to resemble a tight bud, with crumpled ball at base of bud. Wrap floral wire around base of bud, securing paper. Trace pattern for rose petal seven times onto tissue paper; cut out seven petals. Add petals all around bud, one at a time, with straight bottom edges even with base of bud; wrap with wire to secure. When last petal has been added, make a 3/4-inch stem with length of doubled wire. Wrap base of flower with florist's tape, covering wire; continue down to cover stem. Pull tape taut while wrapping; wrap tightly for a firm, straight stem. Twist stem around tree branch.

German Coffee Cake–An Old Favorite

Preheat oven to 350°. Grease a 9-by-13-inch baking pan.

In a large mixing bowl, cream together margarine and sugar. Add eggs, sour cream, baking soda, and vanilla. Beat in flour and baking powder. Stir in nuts.

Pour half of batter into prepared pan. Sprinkle half of topping over batter; run a knife once through batter. Pour remaining batter into the pan, then run a knife once through batter.

Bake until a toothpick inserted into the center comes out clean, approximately 40 to 45 minutes.

Transfer baking pan onto a wire rack. Cool 30 minutes.

1 cup margarine, softened

2 cups granulated sugar

4 large eggs, at room temperature

1 pint sour cream

2 teaspoons baking soda

2 teaspoons vanilla extract

1 1/2 cups all-purpose flour

3 teaspoons baking powder

1/2 cup walnuts

Topping

Mix together 1/2 cup granulated sugar and 2 teaspoons cinnamon.

CHAPTER SIX

Christ Child Lullaby

CHRIST CHILD LULLABY

My love, my pride, my treasure
Oh, My wonder new and pleasure
Oh, My son, my beauty ever you,
Who am I to bear you here?

The cause of talk and tale am I,
The cause of greatest fame am I,
The cause of proudest care on high
To have for mine the King of all.

And though you are the King of all,
They sent you to the manger stall,
Where at your feet they all shall fall
And glorify my child, the King.

There shone a star above three kings
To guide them to the King of Kings,
They held you in their humble arms
And knelt before you until dawn.

They gave you myrrh and gave you gold,
Drank incense and gifts untold.
They traveled far these gifts to bring
And glorify their newborn King.

GAELIC CHRISTMAS SONG

The Manger Was Empty

He arrived early on Christmas morning to give the church a thorough inspection, noting with approval that the aisles and seats had been swept and dusted after the midnight Christmas Eve service. Any lost purses, Bibles, and gloves had been collected and sent to the office where the lost and found box was kept; every forgotten flyer and bulletin insert had been rounded up and discarded.

Outside it was just beginning to grow light. In the church, where only the pastor moved, candles flickered and threw shifting shadows on the arches and the stone floor. Occasionally, stray candlelight picked out the rich colors in the stained glass windows. It was cold and, except for the pastor's slow tread, it was silent.

He paused beside the almost life-sized nativity scene to say a Christmas prayer of thanksgiving to the One whose birth is celebrated. The figures, each lovingly crafted with wonderful realism, sat on a small stage. A night sky and the star that led the shepherds and the wise men to the Messiah on the day of His birth could be seen through the open door of the stable. The shepherds were just entering, eyes wide in obvious awe. Various kinds of livestock stood in stalls or lay on the edges of the scene. And in the center was the Holy Family. Looking at the manger scene, the pastor could almost feel the reverence of that long ago night.

Slowly, a puzzled frown crept across his brow. Then his choked gasp rustled through the empty church.

The manger was empty! The small figure representing the infant Savior was gone.

Hurriedly, and with growing agitation, the pastor began to search the church again. Starting by the manger, he peered back through the aisles, nearly crawling on his hands and knees to see all the way under each seat. But there was nothing. Next, he called the custodian, thinking he may have seen the figure of the infant Jesus. Then he called the assistant pastor and all the elders, but no one had any explanation. In the end, each shaking his head sorrowfully, they accepted the truth they had all been trying to avoid: The figure could not have been mislaid or lost—it must have been stolen.

With solemnity befitting the occasion, the pastor reported the theft to the congregation that assembled not long after. His voice trembled as he told them what he had found earlier that morning. For a person to steal the very symbol of their reason for celebrating, he said, their very reason for hope—well, he just did not understand. His gaze swept over the faces in the early morning congregation, disappointed to think someone in his own congregation might do such a thing.

"The figure of the Christ Child," he said, "must be returned before this Christmas Day is over. No one will ask any questions, but it must be brought back immediately." Then, he slipped from the pulpit and the choir closed the service with a Christmas hymn, "Come, Let Us Adore Him."

The manger remained empty throughout the day.

Toward the end of the afternoon, discouraged and heavy-hearted, the pastor took a walk through the wintry streets of the neighborhood. Ahead of him he saw one of the youngest members of his flock, a six-year-old boy named Tommy. Bundled shabbily against the cold, Tommy trudged up the sidewalk, proudly dragging behind him a toy express wagon. It was bright and red and obviously Christmas-new.

Knowing what sacrifice and scrimping the purchase of this toy must have meant—Tommy's family could barely make ends meet—the pastor was deeply touched. The love Tommy's parents had for their little boy gave the pastor's heart a gentle warmth, and he felt his faith in human nature beginning to return. He sped up so he could wish Tommy a merry Christmas and admire the beautiful new wagon.

But as he drew nearer he saw that the wagon was not empty—there lay the baby Jesus, now wrapped and blanketed but not quite hidden.

The pastor crouched down beside Tommy, one knee feeling the damp snow through his pant leg. His face was grim and disappointed. Tommy may be just a little boy, and one must make allowances of course—but he was still old enough to understand that stealing was very wrong. The pastor made this crystal clear to Tommy while the little boy stood, his seemingly guiltless clear eyes filling with what the pastor was sure were penitent tears.

"But, Pastor," the small boy quavered when at last the man finished talking, "I didn't steal Jesus. It wasn't like that at all." He paused to swallow hard and wipe a few tears away. "It's just that I've been asking Him for a red wagon as a Christmas present for a long time—and I promised Him that when I got it I'd take Him out for the first ride."

—RETOLD BY CASANDRA LINDELL
FROM *CHRISTMAS STORIES FOR THE HEART*

HOLIDAY PRESENTS

She had a splendid Christmas. She went to bed early, so as to let Santa Claus have a chance at the stockings, and in the morning she was up the first of anybody and went and felt them, and found hers all lumpy with packages of candy, and oranges and grapes, and pocketbooks and rubber balls and all kinds of small presents, and her big brother's with nothing but the tongs in them, and her young lady sister's with a new silk umbrella, and her papa's and mama's with potatoes and pieces of coal wrapped up in tissue paper, just as they always had every Christmas. Then she waited around till the rest of the family were up, and she was the first to burst into the library, when the doors were opened, and look at the large presents laid out on the library table—books, and portfolios, and boxes of stationery, and breastpins, and dolls, and little stoves, and dozens of handkerchiefs, and ink stands, and skates, and snow shovels, and photograph frames, and little easels, and boxes of watercolors, and Turkish paste, and nougat, and candied cherries, and dolls' houses, and waterproofs—and the big Christmas tree lighted and standing in a waste basket in the middle.

She had a splendid Christmas all day. She ate so much candy that she did not want any breakfast; and the whole forenoon the presents kept pouring in that the expressman had not had time to deliver the night before; and she went 'round giving the presents she had got for other people, and came home and ate turkey and cranberry for dinner, and plum pudding and nuts and raisins and oranges and more candy, and then went out and coasted and came in with a stomach-ache, crying . . .

—WILLIAM DEAN HOWELLS
FROM *CHRISTMAS EVERY DAY*

This, Too, I Shall Give

In a little town in Florida there was an unpretentious home for small, unwanted boys. Having little of this world's goods, the kindly matron made it up to them the best way she knew how. She loved them, mothered them, fed them, spanked them, taught them to love God, to read their Bibles (those old enough to read, that is), to say their prayers. She laughed with them, listened sympathetically to their troubles (even while she stirred the soup), made her corrections few, her exhortations brief, and loved them some more.

One day—this is a true story—a well-to-do lady from a distant city came to see about adopting a boy. Everyone was pleased and happy for the fortunate little boy who was going to have such a fine home—such a successful man for a father and such a beautifully dressed, bejeweled, and befurred lady for a mother.

The lady smiled down at the small boy and asked, "Do you have a bicycle?"

"No, ma'am."

"Well," she promised, "we will buy you one. And have you roller skates?"

"An old pair," he replied.

"We'll buy you a lovely new pair. And tell me, have you a transistor radio?"

The boy looked puzzled. "I haven't got any radio at all," he said.

"Well, never mind, we'll get you one."

Still puzzled, the small boy studied her solemnly, then blurted, "Please, ma'am, if that's all you're going to give me, I'd rather stay here."

This is the Christmas season, a time for the giving and the receiving of gifts. So it has been—since the Wise Men brought their gold and frankincense and myrrh to the Christ Child.

For weeks now, we've been working on our gift list and shopping, shopping, shopping.

Perhaps skis for that strapping son . . . a negligee for mother . . . that heirloom bracelet for the daughter who has admired it for so long . . . a leather lounge chair for your husband . . . choice books . . . home-baked fruitcake . . . and if you've selected his-and-her airplanes or his-and-her submarines from the gift catalog, we'll add them to the list, too.

In this brief interlude before the final rush, let's pause and hear again the small boy's puzzled question:

"Is that all you're going to give?"

"Is that all!" you ask. Your budget is knocked into a cocked hat already. "What do you mean, 'Is that all?!'"

Just that. "Is that all?"

I'm sure you remember the story of the hoodlums who broke into a department store one night; but it bears retelling. They didn't steal or destroy anything. They just had a wonderful time switching price tags. The next morning customers were puzzled and delighted to find fur coats selling for $5. Cold cream was priced at $150. A silver service was marked $1.75 and a pair of ladies' hose $390. There were umbrellas for $1,000 and diamond rings for $2.

Has something come into our lives and switched the price tags? Are things of time of more value than things of eternity? Are material gifts worth more than gifts of the spirit?

Do we place high price tags on the community rather than on the family? On personal pleasures rather than the needs of those we love? On a TV program rather than family prayers?

When our husbands ask more of us, do we offer a leather lounge chair instead?

When our children long for love and sympathy, do we put them off with a pair of roller skates?

Let me then offer for our consideration a revised shopping list:

This Christmas I am giving my parents more loving appreciation for the years of time and effort—yes, and money—which they invested in me, so much of which I took for granted. I will take time to do the little things to give them pleasure—to give us pleasure together—in the few years I may still have them with me.

To my neighbors—nice or not—I will give thoughtful consideration. I will be slow to gossip, quick to sympathize, ready to help, praying all the while that God will give them the necessary patience to live next to me.

To those who help me in the home I will be quick to praise, slow to blame. I will look for little ways to make their tasks easier, thinking, "Suppose I were in their place." And when my pocketbook permits, a raise. But raise or no raise, praise.

To those who serve me in restaurants or shops—grumpy or obliging, taciturn or otherwise—I will be courteous, friendly, interested, remembering: If I worked so long for so little, if my back ached and my feet hurt, and if when I got home I still had supper to get, I too would be grumpy, taciturn or otherwise.

To all I meet—remembering that each carries burdens known only to himself, and some too big to cope with—I will say the kind things I want (but hesitate) to say. I will tell them the nice things I've heard about them. I will express my appreciation warmly. If there's nothing nice to say, I'll do more than keep my mouth shut sweetly; I'll find something.

To my husband—remembering how much he has had to put up with and for how long—I will give a frank, honest reappraisal of myself. I will ask myself, "If I were my husband, what sort of woman would I want to come home to?" (Every man being different, each of you will have to figure that one out for yourself.)

I will remember that happy marriages don't just happen. They are the result of good hard work. "A happy marriage," as the late Robert Quillen wrote, "is the union of two good forgivers."

Then I will take my Bible and reread those timeworn, ageless passages that speak of love and marriage and the responsibilities and privileges of wives. Sensible, delightful, down-to-earth passages, which if any woman would follow would make her husband the happiest, most contented man on earth.

And all that I give my husband will benefit my children, too.

For, as Dr. David Goodman writes in *A Parent's Guide to the Emotional Needs of Children*, "What a child needs most is two parents who love and appreciate one another and who love and appreciate him. All-round love and appreciation give a family serenity, security, strength."

To my children also this Christmas, I will be more articulate in my love and my appreciation of them as persons. If I cannot give them a perfect mother, I can at least give them more of the one they've got—and make that one more loving. I will be available, knowing that a mother needs, like God, to be "a very present help in trouble." I will take time to listen, time to play (remembering, "You can do anything with a child if only you play with him"). Time to be home when they arrive from school, time to counsel and encourage.

In a world of confusion and uncertainties, I will give them the eternal verities of the Word of God. In a world that has lost its moorings, I will try to help them cast their anchors while they are young on the goodness and mercy of God. In a scientific age, I will teach them the importance of faith. In a day of shifting morals, I will teach them the unchanging absolutes of the Ten Commandments. At a time when aimlessness has become a way of life, I will teach them that man's chief end is still "to glorify God and to enjoy Him forever."

This is the revised list. But the giving has outgrown the giver.

How can we give what we do not have?

How can we purchase what is priceless?

For these are gifts of the heart and of the spirit—timeless and eternal.

All I know is there are those I love who long for (and desperately need) these gifts this Christmas—and my spiritual bank account is zero and there is nothing in savings.

Do you feel that way? Or perhaps you don't even care anymore. Perhaps love is dead. Perhaps the children are already beyond your influence. Perhaps there are no children. Something has happened and there is no real joy or meaning to life anymore. The most you look for is some temporary form of escape.

You can't give. There's nothing left to give. In fact, there's no one left to give to.

Listen.

What's Christmas all about anyway?

Wasn't there a death, an emptiness, a need? Wasn't there a Love somewhere—infinite, eternal, unchangeable—a Love that gave His only Son?

That's what Christmas is all about.

God coming to earth in the person of the Christ Child to do for you and me what we could not possibly do for ourselves. He lived among us and shared our problems for thirty-three years. You haven't a problem, and I haven't a problem, that He doesn't understand from close personal experience. He spent His entire life meeting human needs, ending it on a cross to deal once and for all with man's greatest need—the sin problem. Just before returning to heaven the risen Christ gave us this glorious promise: "Lo, I am with you always."

That's what Christmas is all about.

While He was here on earth Jesus invited men to come to Him: tired men, bad men, good men, bewildered men, laborers, revolutionaries, cheats, bigots. It is the Invitation of the Ages.

Today we come in the same way that they came two thousand years ago, just the way we are. Our only credentials: our need.

Mommie," a small child asked one Christmas, "isn't this Jesus' birthday?"

"Yes," replied the mother.

"Then why," the child wondered, "why do we give presents to everybody else?"

Why?

Because the Christian world remembers—however confusedly, however commercially—that this is the Advent season, a time for joyous giving.

But we have confused the real gifts with the material ones. We have our price tags mixed.

Still the small child's question is valid. What can we give, who have so little to offer? Ourselves.

Remember, that's what God loves so much. All He asks this Christmas is you. You, with your failures, your sins, your problems, your fears. You.

This is Christmas—the real meaning of it.

God loving; searching; giving Himself—to us.

Man needing; receiving; giving himself—to God.

Redemption's glorious exchange of gifts! Without which we cannot live; without which we cannot give to those we love anything of lasting value.

This is the meaning of Christmas—the wonder and the glory of it.

This, too, I shall give.

—RUTH BELL GRAHAM
DECISION, DECEMBER 1965

Cranberry Scones

1 cup dairy sour cream

2 1/2 teaspoons grated fresh orange peel

2 cups sifted all-purpose flour

2 teaspoons baking powder

1/2 teaspoon baking soda

1/2 cup granulated sugar

1 1/2 teaspoons salt

1/4 cup butter or margarine, softened

1 large egg, at room temperature

1/4 cup dried cranberries

Preheat oven to 375°.

In a small bowl, combine sour cream and grated orange peel. Set aside.

In a large bowl, mix together the flour, baking powder, baking soda, granulated sugar, and salt.

Using a pastry blender or two knives held together, cut butter or margarine into the flour mixture until coarse crumbs form.

Break the egg in a small dish and beat well with a fork. Add the egg to the flour mixture and beat together until blended.

Add the sour cream and orange peel mixture and beat until just well blended.

Prepare a smooth surface (the kitchen counter is fine) by sprinkling it lightly with flour. Turn the dough out of the bowl. Using floured hands, knead the dough for about 30 seconds, or until smooth.

Take half the dough; roll it out with a floured rolling pin until it is about half an inch thick. Using a 3-inch round cookie cutter, or even the opening to a similarly sized empty can, cut out rounds of dough. Place the rounds 1 inch apart on a greased or non-stick cookie sheet. Before putting them in the oven, push 5 dried cranberries into the top of each one. Repeat with the remaining dough.

Bake until the tops are just barely browned, 12 to 18 minutes.

Let cool on wire racks. Makes 1 dozen scones.

—FROM *THE EVERYTHING CHRISTMAS BOOK*

Christmas Hearts

For each heart you need two pieces of paper of different colors. They must be three times as long as they are wide. The two pieces are placed on top of each other and folded. Then they are cut together to form two equal-sized, oblong pieces that are closed on one end. Draw lines to follow for cutting the three "ribs." Cut along these lines to form the ribs so they become a little longer than the width of the paper (see line in drawing 1). Draw the rounded line using a compass or a cup, and cut out.

Now you have two identical parts. It is very important that they are exactly alike, otherwise you will have problems weaving them together. Cut out a handle, too.

Now start weaving. Pull the upper-most piece A (see drawing 3) around D, through E and around F. Push it in as far as possible. Then push piece B through D, around E and through F. Weave piece C in the same way as piece A.

With luck, the heart can now be opened like a basket. Glue the handle on the interior of each side, and your basket is ready to hang on the tree.

— KATHLEEN STOKKER
FROM *KEEPING CHRISTMAS:
YULETIDE TRADITIONS IN NORWAY
AND THE NEW LAND*

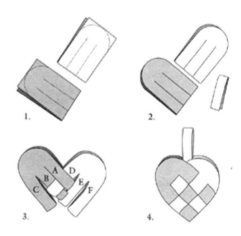

A QUIET KNOWING CHRISTMAS

CHAPTER SEVEN

Away in a Manger

AWAY IN A MANGER

Away in a manger, no crib for a bed,
The little Lord Jesus lay down his sweet head.
The stars in the sky looked down where he lay,
The little Lord Jesus, asleep on the hay.

The cattle are lowing, the baby awakes,
But little Lord Jesus, no crying he makes.
I love thee, Lord Jesus, look down from the sky,
And stay by my cradle till morning is nigh.

Be near me, Lord Jesus, I ask thee to stay
Close by me forever, and love me, I pray.
Bless all the dear children in thy tender care,
And fit us for heaven to live with thee there.

—TRADITIONAL AMERICAN CAROL

The Story of "Away in a Manger"

No Christmas song is more loved than this tender children's carol. With its simply worded expression of love for the Lord Jesus and trust in His faithful care, the hymn appeals to young and old alike. It is usually one of the first Christmas songs learned in early childhood. Almost without exception, every child responds to this text and music, and its pleasing melody and gentle message preserve it in our affections all through life.

For some time, "Away in a Manger" was titled "Luther's Cradle Hymn." It was thought to have been written by Martin Luther for his own children and then passed on by German mothers. Modern research discounts this claim, however. Verses one and two first appeared in the *Little Children's Book*, published in 1885, listing the author as "Anonymous." Two years later the carol appeared in a collection titled *Dainty Songs for Little Lads and Lasses* by James R. Murray, who apparently also composed the familiar tune. Murray was an American music teacher and music publisher. The precious prayer, "Be near me, Lord Jesus," was added several years later by a Methodist minister, Dr. John T. McFarland, for use at a children's Christmas program. Despite the uncertainty of its origin, this charming carol never fails to impress us with the true meaning of Bethlehem's humble manger.

How important it is that we take time to help our children see beyond the glitter and gifts of the Christmas season and to teach them the true meaning of Christ's birth. The most thrilling story ever known began in Bethlehem's manger some two thousand years ago.

—KENNETH OSBECK
FROM *JOY TO THE WORLD: THE STORIES BEHIND YOUR FAVORITE CHRISTMAS CAROLS*

A Christmas Crime

I first discovered F. W. Boreham while reading his book Quest for Serenity. Then I learned that this Australian had written more than fifty books (of which I have collected all but two). I never had the pleasure of meeting him, but Bill met Boreham when he was in Australia and described him as a big man with very large, bony hands. Boreham asked Bill to kneel, and he placed those large, bony hands on him and prayed for him.

—RUTH BELL GRAHAM

This is a story, not of a rapturous Christmastime, nor of a melodious Christmas chime, nor of a lyrical Christmas rhyme, but of a most romantic Christmas crime.

"Have you moved the goose from the woodshed?" We were just sitting down to breakfast on Christmas Eve when our hostess entered the room, and, focusing an anxious scrutiny upon her husband's face, propounded this most unexpected and most disconcerting question.

Amidst tumultuous excitement, the handsome and appetizing bird had, the previous evening, arrived in a crate from an upcountry farm. A letter received earlier in the week had apprised the family of its dispatch, and, from that hour, the three boys—Jack, Ron and Keith—had haunted the railway station like uneasy spirits. Immediately upon the arrival of a train, from whatever direction, they plied the harassed porters with eager enquiries concerning the feverishly expected goose. And when at last, to the infinite relief of the officials, the package duly appeared, the trio dashed off home at breakneck speed to report the sensational arrival. In a few moments, their father drove them back to the station in the car, and the goose was borne triumphantly home. The family having resolved, after a solemn conclave, to defer the execution until the morning, the traveler was released from its crate and imprisoned in the woodshed for the night.

This all happened during our stay at The Pines at Oterakani in New Zealand. As everybody in that romantic neighborhood knows, the Humes are most delightful people. Frederick Hume was the leading solicitor in the town; at the time of our visit, he was mayor of the municipality and has since represented the district in Parliament. He was, moreover, an elder of the Presbyterian Church and a natural leader in all the best movements among the people. Tall, dark, and handsome, with fine eyes, clean, athletic figure and strikingly molded face, he somehow impressed everybody with the feeling that he was in complete control of the situation, whatever that situation might happen to be. His very presence commanded confidence and respect, and his wife exquisitely matched his charm. The Pines, a massive and substantial building standing well back from the road and picturesquely surrounded by graceful lawns and flowering shrubs, is easily the most striking and beautiful home in that part of New Zealand. It is scarcely surprising, therefore, that the fortnight during which we luxuriated in its hospitality is treasured in our memories as one of the choicest and most notable of life's experiences.

The three boys—the eldest eleven, the youngest seven—stared at each other in blank astonishment. For them the earth had suddenly ceased to revolve. The goose not in the woodshed! It was of no use proceeding with breakfast: appetites were in ruins. Like a jury in an important case, we adjourned to inspect the scene of the tragedy. Only two theories were admissible; the goose had somehow escaped of its own accord or it had been maliciously stolen. As, with the shed shut up, the only avenues of escape appeared to be the chinks between the boards and the crack 'round the door, the first of these theories commanded scant support.

Driven perforce to the alternative conclusion, the boys consulted their legal adviser as to the maximum penalty that could be imposed on a thief who stole a goose on Christmas Eve. They themselves cherished a profound conviction that, for their personal delectation, the culprit should be hanged within sight of their windows as they sat at their gooseless dinner on Christmas Day. Their father, however, foresaw legal difficulties that might deprive them of this alluring entertainment.

Following upon our early morning disturbance, we resumed our seats at the breakfast table, and, in spite of everything, did fair justice to the meal. There was, of course, but one topic of conversation. For a while the discussion concerned itself exclusively with the discovery, arrest and punishment of the thief; but, after many possible lines of action had been suggested and dismissed, Mr. Hume advised his sons to leave that aspect of the matter in expert hands.

"I shall be seeing Superintendent Lewis this morning," he explained, "and I'll mention the matter to him. If anything can be done, you may depend upon it the police will do it."

"Well, then," declared Ron, "I'm going to have a good search! The goose may have got out: you never know. I've seen workmen leave their tools and things in our woodshed to save carrying them up and down the back lane. Somebody may have opened the door like that and let the goose out. I'm going to have a good look, anyhow!"

His brothers were manifestly impressed by Ron's new line of argument and straightway offered to join him in his quest. During the morning, they searched in vain; but, the police having found no evidence of theft, they set out with new zest in the afternoon.

It was getting dusk when Mrs. Hume, looking anxiously from the front windows for some sign of her boys, beheld an extraordinary spectacle. The gate was suddenly flung wide open, and the boys, struggling frantically with the goose, entered in boisterous triumph. Ron was tugging at a cord attached to the unhappy bird's foot; Jack, walking beside it, was urging it forward by sundry prods and pushes; whilst little Keith was shooing it on from behind. All three were wildly excited.

"He was down among that clump of gum trees in the empty paddock at the corner of Montagu Street," exclaimed Ron. "My," he continued, "we've had a tussle to get him here."

"Oh, well," laughed their mother, proud of their exploit, "we must get Dad to kill him as soon as we've had dinner; and then everybody must lend a hand with the plucking. We shall have him all ready for Christmas yet!"

We were a very merry party that night. The boys told the story of their adventure repeatedly, and each recital, revealing new details, produced fresh outbursts of laughter. We all did something towards making up for the hours that had been lost; by bedtime the goose was entirely innocent of feathers; and we all crept off to our rooms feeling that the joy of Christmas had been considerably enhanced by the culprit who so carelessly opened the woodshed door.

Next morning, however, the matter assumed a somewhat different aspect. The boys were astir at daylight, investigating the trail that Santa Claus had left. They appeared at breakfast loaded with toys, and wearing tissue-paper caps—a helmet, a miter, and a crown. Then, just as we were rising from the table, Mrs. Hume, glancing at the window, espied the burly form of Superintendent Lewis coming up the drive.

"Well, to be sure!" she exclaimed in astonishment. "Surely he could have left you alone on Christmas Day! Why on earth must he trouble you with Court business this morning?"

"It will be some very little thing," her husband replied soothingly. "I expect he just requires my signature to some document or other. I'll answer the door myself." And off he went. In five minutes he returned, bringing the police officer with him.

"I say," he exclaimed, with a look compounded half of amusement and half of vexation. "Here's a pretty kettle of fish! The Superintendent will tell you all about it."

"Well, ma'am," the officer began, bowing deferentially to Mrs. Hume, "it's like this. Young Mr. and Mrs. Nelson, the newly married couple that live in the redbrick villa near the corner of Montagu Street, had a goose sent them for Christmas, and, thinking it would be perfectly safe, they turned it loose in the vacant paddock next door. It seems that, late last night, Mr. Nelson glanced over the fence to see that it was all right, and found that it had disappeared. He reported it to us first thing this morning; we made enquiries; and—to make a long story short—we soon collected evidence to prove that these three young gentlemen were seen walking off with the missing goose! So I thought I'd better step round and see His Worship about it. He'll know what's best to be done!"

Keith, the youngest of the three brothers, burst into piteous lamentations, haunted, very possibly, by the prospect of spending Christmas Day in the cells. He may even have conjured up the vision—based on their overnight imaginings—of the three youthful thieves being hanged in front of the Nelson windows as the bride and bridegroom sat at their gooseless board. His brothers also looked distressingly glum, foreseeing, as the least of the dire consequences that must swiftly ensue, the loss of their own magnificent goose. Meanwhile, Mr. and Mrs. Hume, having withdrawn into an alcove, were engrossed in a whispered but earnest consultation.

"Oh, you couldn't, Fred," I heard my hostess protest. "It's all ready for cooking; for aught I know, it may even be in the oven. How could you send it now? And, besides, we have visitors. What could we possibly offer them for Christmas dinner if you send away the goose? Can't you buy one somewhere for the Nelsons?"

"I'm afraid it's rather too late for that," the Mayor replied, looking as if the entire organization of the municipality had suddenly broken down. "I haven't a notion in which direction to go in search of one; and by the time I got it, and took it to the Nelson's place, it would be of no use for today's dinner. I'll jump into the car, and run round and see them about it! Come on, Superintendent. I'll drop you at your place on the way!"

In less than an hour he was back, laughing immoderately. He had evidently solved the problem to his own complete satisfaction.

"They're the jolliest young couple I've met for years!" he exclaimed, enthusiastically. "They think it the biggest joke that has come to them since they married: they're just splitting their sides over it. I told them that, if they wished it, we'd send it round at once, or even cooked and ready for table; but they wouldn't hear of it. He said that he was mightily relieved at not having had to kill the creature; he'd never done such a thing in his life. And she declared that she scarcely slept a wink the night before last through worrying about the cooking of it. She's a real Briton; you'd love her. She told me that we were not to worry a scrap. She had a lovely ham, she said, and that would perfectly satisfy them. And, as long as they lived, she assured me, every Christmas dinner would be made the merrier by the memory of their first. So what do you think I did—I hope you won't mind."

"Asked them to dinner here, I suppose," his wife hazarded, knowing him pretty well.

"Got it right, first guess," he laughed. "Yes, they're coming. I'm to go back for them in an hour's time."

That was one of the merriest Christmases that we spent in New Zealand. The bride and bridegroom entered into the spirit of the thing, and, displaying remarkable versatility, romped with the boys until bedtime. And, after the youngsters had said goodnight, they proved themselves, at the fireside, the most engaging and congenial companions.

Friendships were forged that Christmas Day that the

years have strengthened and sweetened. The following Christmas Day was spent by the Nelsons very differently. There was no question of killing or cooking a goose, for Mrs. Nelson was in bed, proudly pressing to her breast the loveliest Christmas gift that could possibly have come to her. Early in the New Year, Mr. and Mrs. Nelson joined the Church. "It was absolutely the only thing that we could do," the young mother told the old minister when he called to see them about it; "the Humes have made religion seem so beautiful and so wonderful that we simply could not be left out in the cold—especially now that little Nora has come to us."

Twenty years later that same little Nora became the bride of Keith, the youngest of the Hume boys. To this day, the Christmas dinner is the event of the year with them all. From far and near they gather for that Yuletide feast. There is always a goose; and the goose is most carefully chosen and most vigilantly guarded. For the benefit of the younger members of the group, who have no personal recollection of the historic happening, the story of the celebrated adventure is annually recited, amidst appropriate ripples of Christmas merriment. Nobody listens more intently than Nora. Keith has a stock jibe that he whips out whenever he finds himself in the humor to tease his pretty, young wife. "I went out in search of one goose," he will say, "and lo and behold, I caught another." But he wipes out the insult later on by proposing the health of The Man Who Stole the Goose from the Woodshed—a toast that, greeted by the entire company with tremendous enthusiasm, is always drunk with musical honors.

—F.W. BOREHAM
FROM *MY CHRISTMAS BOOK*

BRIGHT STAR SHINING

A star was His night-light,
His quilt was the sky,
And soft sang His mother
In case He should cry,

And all the brown cattle
Came close to His bed
To see the small Baby
Asleep in their shed.

His carols were praises
Of love and goodwill,
That rose in the midnight
So clear and so still,

To herald the earliest
Christmas we know,
When Jesus was little,
A long time ago.

—ELIZABETH FLEMING
FROM *POEMS FOR CHRISTMAS*

Christmas Kitchen Fifty Years Ago

Our old kitchen returns in my memory, decked out in its winter ways. Always, as I think about it, a fire burns easy and slow in the fireplace, and one of the cats is asleep at its edge; and somebody, Big Granny or Mother or the cook, is rocking in the chair near the cat with a pan on her lap preparing something for dinner or supper.

The kitchen was a big wide room on the southwest side of the house, full of yellow light in the afternoon; and this yellow light always smelled like spice cake, or spareribs slowly browning, or maybe sweet potato pies at the crusty moment of being considered "done" and ready to set out on a long table to cool.

In the big black iron stove was a murmur of wood burning in slow steady combustion, just right for the pies. A wood box was at the side of the stove stacked with various kinds of wood: resinous kindling for a sudden flame, splintered dry pine for a quick breakfast fire, a little green pine to temper the dry pine, oak split into the proper size and length for the long haul of the four-hour roasting which a fresh ham requires.

In this cavernous, bright, spice-laden kitchen the Christmas preparations began in late November, for the fruitcakes were always made early and set aside in the dark pantry to season.

I don't see how my mother could have managed without the big enameled dishpans at such a time. She'd sit at the wide table alongside Big Granny or Little Granny and the cook cutting orange peel and raisins, citron and ginger and pecans, until one of the pans would be filled with the sticky, spicy mess. Then she would measure into another pan flour by the quart and sugar by the pint. She'd leave this, go to the pantry, and return with a basket filled with six or seven dozen eggs. I liked the creamy brown ones best and would ask to be permitted to count out the two dozen needed. Then Mother would break them, giving each a sharp nip on the edge of the table, and deposit their undisturbed contents, freed of the shells, into the pan. The whole affair was elegant: golden orbs of eggs floating in islands of white . . . Mother's quick, dexterous movements as she went about her work . . . everything calmly moving toward her completion. She was an artist in her own kitchen, and there was a deep pleasure in her eyes as she gently pushed prying little ones away, and went on with her creation.

The day came when I had my try at breaking an egg—something which, somewhere in me, had become almost as taboo as setting fire to the house or flinging one of her Haviland china plates to the floor. But now I was seven and grown up enough, and Mother gave her permission to try. I stood trembling for five minutes on the edge of that precipice before I took the fatal step. But I took it. I cracked the egg. Then hesitating again, I brought on disaster by spilling the egg on the floor. But Mother did not scold: she said, "It happens; let's clean it up." We cleaned it up. Then she said, "Try again." And I tried again, and I did it. And I am not sure any triumph in my life ever pleased me more than that successful act.

Now, over the fruit and nuts, were sprinkled cinnamon and nutmeg and mace and a little grated lemon peel. The nuts and fruit and flour and sugar and eggs were finally mixed well together in the biggest pan of all. Someone had greased the four-inch-deep cake pans and lined them with brown paper and now they were filled and placed in shallow biscuit tins lined with a half-inch of water for the slow steam-baking they required.

But for me, the making of fruitcake never quite reached the mouth-watering excitement of watching our mother do her famous turkey dressing. To experience this involved your glands, senses, mind, heart, and soul.

It took place on Christmas morning. And no matter how absorbed I might be with new dolls and new books I'd be on hand to witness this great spectacle:

First, she crushed the contents of a dozen or more boxes of Uneeda Biscuits in a deep bowl. On these crushed crackers she poured the "essence," which had resulted from browning and simmering for two hours the neck, liver, gizzard, and wing tips of the twenty-eight-pound turkey. If the essence did not dampen the crackers sufficiently—and it never did—she then "stole," as she said, three or four cups of the most delicious-smelling stock from the turkey roasting pan and added it to the mixture. This stealing always sent me into giggles, but I'd keep glancing up at her face to be sure she was joking; for unlike my father, she joked rarely, and when she did, she joked so dryly that we were never quite sure she meant it as a joke. Anyway, after the theft of the turkey stock, she added six or seven cups of finely chopped celery, a few celery seeds, salt, pepper, a little chopped onion (not much), a half-pound of homemade butter (depending on the richness of the essence), and two dozen eggs. This was well stirred, then two quarts of pecans were added, and two quarts of oysters and a cupful or so of oyster liquor. The whole thing was now stirred for five minutes or more, tasted, a little sage added, a mite more pepper, and then after staring hard at it, Mother would go to the stove, pick up the kettle, and pour a bit of steaming water into the pan to soften it a little more. This was IT. Mother then pushed some of it into the turkey pan—not much, for the turkey was cooking and already had a sausage stuffing in it. Then, after looking at it again for a long moment, and tasting it once more, she poured this delicious mess into deep baking dishes and set it aside to be cooked for thirty or forty minutes shortly before dinner. When served, it would be firm but fluffy, with just enough crispy bits of pecans and succulent oysters.

By this time, the big sisters had filled silver dishes with candies and nuts and stuffed dates, and glass dishes were filled with homemade pickles and olives; somebody was stuffing the celery with cheese and someone else was easing the jellied cranberry sauce onto one of Mother's fancy fluted porcelain dishes. The cook, or perhaps Big Grandma, had prepared the sweet potatoes for candying, and they were now on the back of the stove gently simmering in water, sugar, butter, orange peel, and cinnamon. The rice would be cooked during the last twenty-two minutes before the dinner bell was rung, but already the gravy had been made and thickened with chopped liver, gizzard, and hard-boiled eggs.

The pork salad and Waldorf salad, made early, were kept in the ice-cold pantry until just before dinner, when they were placed on the sideboard in two hand-painted bowls. Also on the sideboard were fruitcake, caramel cake, six-layered coconut cake, Lord Baltimore cake, lemon cheesecake, and several coconut pies. Our father always ate a slice of coconut pie, but the rest of us preferred the traditional ambrosia for Christmas dessert, with a sampling of all the cakes.

Since the Greeks there have been ambrosias and ambrosias. Ours was fit for the most exacting Olympian taste, for it was of a special delicacy since the oranges were not sliced, but each plug of fruit lifted out of its inner skin and kept as nearly whole as possible. A layer of these fragile orange plugs would be put in a bowl, then a layer of finely grated fresh coconut (not shredded), then a sprinkling of sugar, then another layer of orange, coconut, and so on, until the bowl was full. It might have tasted better served to you as you reclined on a floating cloud, but I doubt it.

And then, the dinner bell rang, and in we ran, already too stuffed by our nibblings since five A.M. to do more than admire, sniff, and taste here and there. But no matter how poked out I was, I made a miracle somehow and pushed in two helpings of turkey dressing. The other things could wait until tomorrow or the next day or the next.

The Famous Turkey Dressing

"Christmas Fifty Years Ago"

We made it in my childhood with Uneeda Biscuits, but I find unsalted, crisp plain crackers of any brand as good.

For six people, four cups of crushed crackers should be sufficient. Boil neck, liver, gizzard (after browning in a little butter) for at least two hours or until tender; add water now and then, if necessary. You should have two cups of strong stock, seasoned with salt and pepper and two stalks of celery. Remove the celery and add stock to the crackers. Then add two cups of diced fresh celery, one cup of nuts, one cup of oysters. A half-cup of oyster liquor will improve this mixture. Chip a small amount of onion—no more than half a teaspoonful—add a skimpy bit of garlic (if you like) but no more than a bare suggestion (one half a small clove, chipped). Add a pinch of thyme, a pinch of sage. I usually add a few sliced ripe olives and a few mushrooms, which I think enhance the flavor. Now, as did my mother, "steal" a little rich stock out of the turkey pan, as much as you can spare, taking care that you leave plenty for gravy. Add three eggs and stir several minutes. You should now have a soft, but not soupy, mixture. If you do not, add a bit of hot water. Or if too soupy, add a slice of broken-up bread, or a few more crackers. Now put in as much butter as your family's health can take. A large tablespoon is plenty for my modern taste. It should melt in the warm mixture as you stir.

The dressing is ready now for your casseroles and should fill two small ones or one large one. Let it stand an hour, then cook 30 minutes; keep warm for dinner.

—LILLIAN SMITH
FROM *MEMORY OF A LARGE CHRISTMAS*

Decorations from the Kitchen

*Kitchen materials can help you come up with
some unique Christmas decorations—some of them edible!
Here is one idea:*

Tie up some cinnamon sticks with a holiday bow; place this on the stove or on the mantel. The fragrance is lovely, and the look is one of old-fashioned charm.

—FROM *THE EVERYTHING CHRISTMAS BOOK*

A QUIET KNOWING CHRISTMAS

CHAPTER EIGHT

Oh, Tannenbaum

OH, TANNENBAUM

O Christmas tree, O Christmas tree,
With faithful leaves unchanging;
Not only green in summer's heat,
But also winter's snow and sleet.
O Christmas tree, O Christmas tree,
With faithful leaves unchanging;

O Christmas tree, O Christmas tree,
Of all the trees most lovely;
Each year, you bring to me delight
Gleaming in the Christmas night.
O Christmas tree, O Christmas tree,
Of all the trees most lovely;

O Christmas tree, O Christmas tree,
Your leaves will teach me, also.
That hope and love and faithfulness
Are precious things I can possess.
O Christmas tree, O Christmas tree,
Your leaves will teach me, also.

— GERMAN SONG

Martin Luther and the First Christmas Tree

One clear cold Christmas Eve the famous Reformation leader Martin Luther was walking home through the woods. As it was a beautiful starry night, he paused for a moment to gaze at the sky in reverent meditation. He was in a grove of tall pines. Their fragrance reminded him of incense and the peaceful murmur of the wind in their branches sounded like a congregation at prayer. From where he stood it seemed as though the thousands of stars had settled on their branches.

He proceeded to cut a tiny tree and took it home where he decorated it with small candles in metal holders to re-create his experience for his children. That glittering tree became a tradition for his family in the many Christmases to come just as it has for many other families around the world.

—Sheryl Ann Karas
from *The Solstice Evergreen: The History, Folklore and Origins of the Christmas Tree*

A Christmas Tree

I have been looking at a merry company of children assembled round that pretty German toy, a Christmas Tree. The tree was planted in the middle of a great round table, and towered high above their heads. It was brilliantly lighted by a multitude of little tapers; and everywhere sparkled and glittered with bright objects. There were rosy-cheeked dolls, hiding behind the green leaves; and there were real watches (with movable hands, at least, and an endless capacity of being wound up) dangling from innumerable twigs; there were French-polished tables, chairs, bedsteads, wardrobes, eight-day clocks, and various other articles of domestic furniture (wonderfully made in tin), perched among the boughs, as if in preparation for some fairy housekeeping; there were jolly, broad-faced little men, much more agreeable in appearance than many real men—and no wonder, for their heads took off, and showed them to be full of sugar-plums; there were trinkets for the elder girls, far brighter than any grown-up gold and jewels; there were baskets and pin cushions in all devices; there were guns, swords, and banners; there were witches standing in enchanted rings of pasteboard, to tell fortunes; there were teetotums, humming-tops, needlecases, pen-wipers, smelling-bottles, conversation-cards, bouquet-holders; real fruit, made artificially dazzling with gold leaf; imitation apples, pears, and walnuts, crammed with surprises; in short, as a pretty child, before me, delightedly whispered to another pretty child, her bosom friend, "There was everything, and more."

—CHARLES DICKENS
FROM *HOUSEHOLD WORDS*

My First Christmas Tree

Pulitzer Prize–winning writer Hamlin Garland, born in 1860, grew up on a farm in the Midwest before heading east to write for Boston and New York newspapers. This scene takes place in the 1870s in Wisconsin.

— RUTH BELL GRAHAM

I will begin by saying that we never had a Christmas tree in our house in the Wisconsin coulee; indeed, my father never saw one in a family circle till he saw that which I set up for my own children last year. But we celebrated Christmas in those days, always, and I cannot remember a time when we did not all hang up our stockings for "Sandy Claws" to fill. As I look back upon those days it seems as if the snows were always deep, the night skies crystal clear, and the stars especially lustrous with frosty sparkles of blue and yellow fire and probably this was so, for we lived in a Northern land where winter was usually stern and always long.

I recall one Christmas when "Sandy" brought me a sled, and a horse that stood on rollers—a wonderful tin horse which I very shortly split in two in order to see what his insides were. Father traded a cord of wood for the sled, and the horse cost twenty cents—but they made the day wonderful.

Another notable Christmas Day, as I stood in our front yard, mid-leg deep in snow, a neighbor drove by closely muffled in furs, while behind his seat his son, a lad of twelve or fifteen, stood beside a barrel of apples, and as he passed he hurled a glorious big red one at me. It missed me, but bored a deep, round hole in the soft snow. I thrill yet with the remembered joy of burrowing for that delicious bomb. Nothing will ever smell quite as good as that Wine Sapor Northern Spy or whatever it was. It was a wayward impulse on the part of the boy in the sleigh, but it warms my heart after more than forty years.

We had no chimney in our home, but the stocking-hanging was a ceremony nevertheless. My parents, and especially, my mother, entered into it with the best of humor. They always put up their own stockings or permitted us to do it for them—and they always laughed next morning when they found potatoes or ears of corn in them. I can see now that my mother's laugh had a tear in it, for she loved pretty things and seldom got any during the years that we lived in the coulee.

When I was ten years old we moved to Mitchell County, an Iowa prairie land, and there we prospered in such wise that our stockings always held toys of some sort, and even my mother's stocking occasionally sagged with a simple piece of jewelry or a new comb or brush. But the thought of a family tree remained the luxury of millionaire city dwellers; indeed it was not till my fifteenth or sixteenth year that our Sunday school rose to the extravagance of a tree, and it is of this wondrous festival that I write.

The land about us was only partly cultivated at this time, and our district schoolhouse, a rare little box, was set bleakly on the prairie; but the Burr Oak schoolhouse was not only larger but it stood beneath great oaks as well and possessed the charm of a forest background through which a stream ran silently. It was our chief social center. There of a Sunday a regular preacher held "Divine Service" with Sunday school as a sequence. At night—usually on Friday nights—the young people led in "ly-ceums," as we called them, to debate great questions or to "speak pieces" and read essays; and here it was that I saw my first Christmas tree.

I walked to that tree across four miles of moonlit snow. Snow? No, it was a floor of diamonds, a magical world, so beautiful that my heart still aches with the wonder of it and with the regret that it has all gone—gone with the keen eyes and the bounding pulses of the boy.

Our home at this time was a small frame house on the prairie almost directly west of the Burr Oak grove, and as it was too cold to take the horses out, my brother and I, with our tall boots, our visored caps, and our long woolen mufflers, started forth afoot defiant of the cold. We left the gate on the trot, bound for a sight of the glittering unknown. The snow was deep and we moved side by side in the grooves made by the hooves of the horses, setting our feet in the shine left by the broad shoes of the wood sleighs whose going had smoothed the way for us.

Our breaths rose like smoke in the still air. It must have been ten below zero, but that did not trouble us in those days, and at last we came in sight of the lights, in sound of the singing, the laughter, the bells of the feast.

It was a poor little building without a tower or bell and its low walls had but three windows on a side, and yet it seemed very imposing to me that night as I crossed the threshold and faced the strange people who packed it to the door. I say "strange people," for though I had seen most of them many times they all seemed somehow alien to me that night. I was an irregular attendant at Sunday school and did not expect a present, there-fore I stood against the wall and gazed with open-eyed marveling at the shining pine which stood where the pulpit was wont to be. I was made to feel the more embarrassed by reason of the remark of a boy who accused me of having forgotten to comb my hair.

This was not true, but the cap I wore always matted my hair down over my brow, and then, when I lifted it off invariably disarranged it completely. Nevertheless I felt guilty—and hot. I don't suppose my hair was artistically barbered that night—I rather guess Mother had used the shears—and I can believe that I looked the half-wild colt that I was; but there was no call for that youth to direct attention to my unavoidable shagginess.

I don't think the tree had many candles, and I don't remember that it glittered with golden apples. But it was loaded with presents, and the girls coming and going clothed in bright garments made me forget my own looks—I think they made me forget to remove my overcoat, which was a sodden thing of poor cut and worse quality. I think I must have stood agape for nearly two hours listening to the songs, noting every motion of Adoniram Burtch and Asa Walker as they directed the ceremonies and prepared the way for the great event—that is to say, for the coming of Santa Claus himself.

A furious jingle of bells, a loud voice outside, the lifting of a window, the nearer clash of bells, and the dear old Saint appeared (in the person of Stephen Bartle) clothed in a red robe, a belt of sleigh bells, and a long white beard. The children cried out, "Oh!" The girls tittered and shrieked with excitement, and the boys laughed and clapped their hands. Then "Sandy" made a little speech about being glad to see us all, but as he had many other places to visit, and as there were a great many presents to distribute, he guessed he'd have to ask some of the many pretty girls to help him. So he called upon Betty Burtch and Hattie Knapp—and I for one admired his taste, for they were the most popular maids of the school.

They came up blushing and a little bewildered by the blaze of publicity thus blown upon them. But their native dignity asserted itself, and the distribution of the presents began. I have a notion now that the fruit upon the tree was mostly bags of popcorn and "corny copias" of candy, but as my brother and I stood there that night and saw everybody, even the rowdiest boy, getting something we felt aggrieved and rebellious. We forgot that we had come from afar—we only knew we were being left out.

But suddenly, in the midst of our gloom, my brother's name was called, and a lovely girl with a gentle smile handed him a bag of popcorn. My heart glowed with gratitude. Somebody had thought of us; and when she came to me, saying sweetly, "Here's something for you," I had not words to thank her. This happened nearly forty years ago, but her smile, her outstretched hand, her sympathetic eyes are vividly before me. At last I had to take my final glimpse of that wondrous tree, and I well remember the walk home. My brother and

I traveled in wordless companionship. The moon was sinking toward the west and the snow crust gleamed with a million fairy lamps. The sentinel watchdogs barked from lonely farmhouses, and the wolves answered from the ridges. Now and then sleighs passed us with lovers sitting two and two, and the bells on their horses had the remote music of romance to us whose boots drummed like clogs of wood upon the icy road.

Our house was dark as we approached and entered it, but how deliciously warm it seemed after the pitiless wind! I confess we made straight for the cupboard for a mince pie, a doughnut, and a bowl of milk!

As I write this there stands in my library a thick-branched, beautifully tapering fir tree covered with the gold and purple apples of Hesperides, together with crystal ice points, green and red and yellow candles, clusters of gilded grapes, wreaths of metallic frost, and glittering angels swinging in ecstasy; but I doubt if my children will ever

know the keen pleasure (that is almost pain) which came to my brother and to me in those Christmas days when an orange was not a breakfast fruit, but a casket of incense and of spice, a message from the sunlands of the South.

That was our compensation—we brought to our Christmastime a keen appetite and empty hands. And the lesson of it all is, if we are seeking a lesson, that it is better to give to those who want than to those for whom "we ought to do something because they did something for us last year."

—H A M L I N   G A R L A N D

Popcorn-and-Cranberry Garland

MATERIALS: popcorn, cranberries, needle, heavy thread

DIRECTIONS: Thread a medium-sized needle with 72 inches of heavy thread. Double back and knot the end.

Pass the needle through the center of five pieces of popcorn and then through one cranberry. Repeat this pattern (or a variation of your own) until the string is full.

Remove the needle and knot the end of the thread. The completed garlands may be tied together at the ends to form one long garland.

—FROM "CHRISTMAS IN NEW ENGLAND"
WORLD BOOK ENCYCLOPEDIA

The Peterkins' Christmas Tree

This story reminds me of the Christmas that Bill decided to go out and cut down a tree instead of buying one. But in the forest, a tree looks much smaller than it does inside. He cut what he thought was the perfect tree, but when he brought back to the house, it was twice as tall as the ceiling of the living room. Bill decided to cut it down to size, but instead of cutting it from the bottom, he cut the top off. So on Christmas Eve, chuckling, I went to the nearest tree lot and found a Christmas tree filled with pinecones. It was the prettiest tree we ever had.

—RUTH BELL GRAHAM

Early in the autumn the Peterkins began to prepare for their Christmas tree. Everything was done in great privacy, as it was to be a surprise to the neighbors, as well as to the rest of the family. Mr. Peterkin had been up to Mr. Bromwick's wood-lot, and with his consent, selected the tree. Agamemnon went to look at it occasionally after dark, and Solomon John made frequent visits to it mornings, just after sunrise. Mr. Peterkin drove Elizabeth Eliza and her mother that way, and pointed furtively to it with his whip; but none of them ever spoke of it aloud to each other. It was suspected that the little boys had been to see it Wednesday and Saturday afternoons. But they came home with their pockets full of chestnuts, and said nothing about it.

At length Mr. Peterkin had it cut down and brought secretly into the Larkins' barn. A week or two before Christmas a measurement was made of it with Elizabeth Eliza's yardmeasure. To Mr. Peterkin's great dismay it was discovered that it was too high to stand in the back parlor.

This fact was brought out at a secret council of Mr. and Mrs. Peterkin, Elizabeth Eliza, and Agamemnon.

Agamemnon suggested that it might be set up slanting; but Mrs. Peterkin was very sure it would make her dizzy, and the candles would drip.

But a brilliant idea came to Mr. Peterkin. He proposed that the ceiling of the parlor should be raised to make room for the top of the tree.

Elizabeth Eliza thought the space would need to be quite large. It must not be like a small box, or you could not see the tree.

"Yes," said Mr. Peterkin, "I should have the ceiling lifted all across the room; the effect would be finer."

Elizabeth Eliza objected to having the whole ceiling raised, because her room was over the back parlor, and she would have no floor while the alteration was going on, which would be very awkward. Besides, her room was not very high now, and, if the floor were raised, perhaps she could not walk in it upright.

Mr. Peterkin explained that he didn't propose altering the whole ceiling, but to lift up a ridge across the room at the back part where the tree was to stand. This would make a hump, to be sure, in Elizabeth Eliza's room; but it would go across the whole room.

Elizabeth Eliza said she would not mind that. It

would be like the cuddy thing that comes upon the deck of a ship, that you sit against, only here you would not have the sea-sickness. She thought she should like it, for a rarity. She might use it for a divan.

Mrs. Peterkin thought it would come in the worn place of the carpet, and might be a convenience in making the carpet over.

Agamemnon was afraid there would be trouble in keeping the matter secret, for it would be a long piece of work for a carpenter; but Mr. Peterkin proposed having the carpenter for a day or two, for a number of other jobs.

One of them was to make all the chairs in the house of the same height, for Mrs. Peterkin had nearly broken her spine by sitting down in a chair that she had supposed was her own rocking-chair, and it had proved to be two inches lower. The little boys were now large enough to sit in any chair; so a medium was fixed upon to satisfy all the family, and the chairs were made uniformly of the same height.

On consulting the carpenter, however, he insisted that the tree could be cut off at the lower end to suit the height of the parlor, and demurred at so great a change as altering the ceiling. But Mr. Peterkin had set his mind upon the improvement, and Elizabeth Eliza had cut her carpet in preparation for it.

So the folding-doors into the back parlor were closed, and for nearly a fortnight before Christmas there was great litter of fallen plastering, and laths, and chips, and shavings; and Elizabeth Eliza's carpet was taken up, and the furniture had to be changed, and one night she had to sleep at the Bromwicks', for there was a long hole in her floor that might be dangerous.

All this delighted the little boys. They could not understand what was going on. Perhaps they suspected a Christmas tree, but they did not know why a Christmas tree should have so many chips, and were still more astonished at the hump that appeared in Elizabeth Eliza's room. It must be a Christmas present, or else the tree in a box.

Some aunts and uncles, too, arrived a day or two before Christmas, with some small cousins. These cousins occupied the attention of the little boys, and there was a great deal of whispering and mystery, behind doors, and under the stairs, and in the corners of the entry.

Solomon John was busy, privately making some candles for the tree. He had been collecting some bayberries, as he understood they made very nice candles, so that it would not be necessary to buy any.

The elders of the family never all went into the back parlor together, and all tried not to see what was going on. Mrs. Peterkin would go in with Solomon John, or Mr. Peterkin with Elizabeth Eliza, or Elizabeth Eliza and Agamemnon and Solomon John. The little boys and the small cousins were never allowed even to look inside the room.

Elizabeth Eliza meanwhile went into town a number of times. She wanted to consult Amanda as to how much ice cream they should need, and whether they could make it at home, as they had cream and ice. She was pretty busy in her own room; the furniture had to be changed, and the carpet altered. The "hump" was higher than she expected. There was danger of bumping her own head whenever she crossed it. She had to nail some padding on the ceiling for fear of accidents.

The afternoon before Christmas, Elizabeth Eliza, Solomon John, and their father collected in the back parlor for a council. The carpenters had done their work, and the tree stood at its full height at the back of the room, the top stretching up into the space arranged for it. All the chips and shavings were cleared away, and it stood on a neat box.

But what were they to put upon the tree?

Solomon John had brought in his supply of candles; but they proved to be very "stringy" and very few of them. It was strange how many bayberries it took to make a few candles! The little boys had helped him, and he had gathered as much as a bushel of bayberries. He had put them in water, and skimmed off the wax, according to the directions; but there was so little wax!

Solomon John had given the little boys some of the bits sawed off from the legs of the chairs. He had suggested that they should cover them with gilt paper, to answer for gilt apples, without telling them what they were for.

These apples, a little blunt at the end, and the candles, were all they had for the tree!

After all her trips into town Elizabeth Eliza had forgotten to bring anything for it.

"I thought of candies and sugar-plums," she said, "but I concluded if we made caramels ourselves we should not need them. But, then, we have not made caramels. The fact is, that day my head was full of my carpet. I had bumped it pretty badly, too."

Mr. Peterkin wished he had taken, instead of a fir-tree, an apple-tree he had seen in October, full of red fruit.

"But the leaves would have fallen off by this time," said Elizabeth Eliza.

"And the apples, too," said Solomon John.

"It is odd I should have forgotten, that day I went in on purpose to get the things," said Elizabeth Eliza, musingly. "But I went from shop to shop, and didn't know exactly what to get. I saw a great many gilt things for Christmas trees; but I knew the little boys were making the gilt apples; there were plenty of candles in the shops, but I knew Solomon John was making the candles."

Mr. Peterkin thought it was quite natural.

Solomon John wondered if it were too late for them to go into town now.

Elizabeth Eliza could not go in the next morning, for there was to be a grand Christmas dinner, and Mr. Peterkin could not be spared, and Solomon John was sure he and Agamemnon would not know what to buy. Besides, they would want to try the candles tonight.

Mr. Peterkin asked if the presents

everybody had been preparing would not answer. But Elizabeth Eliza knew they would be too heavy.

A gloom came over the room. There was only a flickering gleam from one of Solomon John's candles that he had lighted by way of trial.

Solomon John again proposed going into town. He lighted a match to examine the newspaper about the trains. There were plenty of trains coming out at that hour, but none going in except a very late one. That would not leave time to do anything and come back.

"We could go in, Elizabeth Eliza and I," said Solomon John, "but we should not have time to buy anything."

Agamemnon was summoned in. Mrs. Peterkin was entertaining the uncles and aunts in the front parlor. Agamemnon wished there was time to study up something about electric lights. If they could only have a calcium light! Solomon John's candle sputtered and went out.

At this moment there was a loud knocking at the front door. The little boys, and the small cousins, and the uncles and aunts, and Mrs. Peterkin hastened to see what was the matter.

The uncles and aunts thought somebody's house must be on fire. The door was opened, and there was a man, white with flakes, for it was beginning to snow, and he was pulling in a large box.

Mrs. Peterkin supposed it contained some of Elizabeth Eliza's purchases, so she ordered it to be pushed into the back parlor, and hastily called back her guests and the little boys into the other room. The little boys and the small cousins were sure they had seen Santa Claus himself.

Mr. Peterkin lighted the gas. The box was addressed to Elizabeth Eliza. It was from the lady from Philadelphia! She had gathered a hint from Elizabeth Eliza's letters that there was to be a Christmas tree, and had filled this box with all that would be needed.

It was opened directly. There was every kind of gilt hanging-thing, from gilt pea-pods to butterflies on springs. There were shining flags and lanterns, and bird-cages, and nests with birds sitting on them, baskets of fruit, gilt apples and bunches of grapes, and, at the bottom of the whole, a large box of candles and a box of Philadelphia bonbons!

Elizabeth Eliza and Solomon John could scarcely keep from screaming. The little boys and the small cousins knocked on the folding-doors to ask what was the matter.

Hastily Mr. Peterkin and the rest took out the things and hung them on the tree, and put on the candles.

When it was all done, it looked so well that Mr. Peterkin exclaimed: "Let us light the candles now, and send to invite all the neighbors tonight, and have the tree on Christmas Eve!"

And so it was the Peterkins had their Christmas tree the day before, and on Christmas night could go and visit their neighbors.

—L U C R E T I A   P .   H A L E

F R O M   *A   C H R I S T M A S   T R E A S U R Y   O F   Y U L E T I D E   A N D   P O E M S*

OUR CHRISTMAS TREE

Our Christmas tree is
not electrified, is not
covered with little lights
calling attention to themselves
(we have had enough
of little lights calling attention
to themselves). Our tree
is a cedar cut here, one
of the fragrances of our place,
hung with painted cones and
paper stars folded
long ago to praise our tree,
Christ come into the world.

—WENDELL BERRY

Wish Cookies—You'll Wish You'd Made More!

10 graham crackers, crushed

¹/₂ cup butter or margarine, melted

¹/₂ cup chopped almonds

6 ounces chocolate chips

¹/₂ cup sweetened shredded coconut

1 can condensed milk

Preheat oven to 350°. In a large mixing bowl, combine melted butter with graham crackers. Mix well. Press crumb mixture into bottom of a 13-by-9-inch pan. Sprinkle nuts, then chocolate chips, and coconut (in that order) over cracker crumbs. Gently pour condensed milk over top. Bake for 15 to 20 minutes or until golden brown. Let cool before cutting.

—FROM *THE EVERYTHING CHRISTMAS BOOK*

A QUIET KNOWING CHRISTMAS

CHAPTER NINE

Silent Night

SILENT NIGHT

Silent night, Holy night,
All is calm, all is bright,
Round yon virgin mother and child,
Holy infant so tender and mild,
Sleep in heavenly peace,
Sleep in heavenly peace.

Silent night, Holy night,
Shepherds quake at the sight;
Glories stream from heaven afar,
Heavenly hosts sing alleluia,
Christ, the savior, is born!
Christ, the savior, is born!

Silent night, Holy night,
son of God, love's pure light
Radiant beams from thy holy face,
With the dawn of redeeming grace,
Jesus, Lord, at thy birth,
Jesus, Lord, at thy birth.

—WORDS BY JOSEPH MOHR, MUSIC BY FRANZ GRUBER
COMPOSED IN AUSTRIA, 1818
ENGLISH TRANSLATION FROM *C. L. HURCHINS'S SUNDAY SCHOOL HYMNAL*

The song "Silent Night" echoed out of the small village of Oberndorf in the Tyrolean Alps of Austria. The twenty-five-year-old rector of the village church, Joseph Mohr, was alone on Christmas Eve, 1818, when he heard a loud pounding on the door. He opened the door and a woman pushed past him gasping, "Come, a child is born, and the young father and mother want you to bless their home." Then the woman collapsed.

The rector started out on a tedious journey up the mountainside, to a small cabin, miles in the distance. After many hours of climbing he reached his destination and saw within the cabin a repetition of the Nativity scene. The young woman lay on a bed of boughs, and her newborn son lay in a roughhewn cradle made by the Alpine-mountaineer father. The rector blessed the home and left the cabin to make a return journey to the village. His heart filled with song, because of the uplifting impressive scene; and his ears filled with the rapturous tune, which enveloped him. Keeping his feet in rhythm he made his way down the mountainside. That Christmas night the rector stayed up writing the manuscript.

The next morning Joseph Mohr visited the village organist and choirmaster, Franz Gruber. He asked the choirmaster to pick out the melody for the song on an old guitar because the organ was broken. A few hours later Franz Gruber ran to the rectory with the tune and the words he had sounded out. On December 25, 1818, the villagers of Oberndorf gathered in the rectory to hear for the first time the song "Silent Night," sung by Joseph Mohr and Franz Gruber. It was a song of peace.

—JOAN WINMILL BROWN
FROM *BEST OF CHRISTMAS JOYS*

CHRISTMAS CAROL

Villagers all, this frosty tide,
Let your doors swing open wide,
Though wind may follow and snow betide
Yet draw us in by your fire to bide:
Joy shall be yours in the morning.

Here we stand in the cold and the sleet,
Blowing fingers and stamping feet,
Come from far away, you to greet
You by the fire and we in the street
Bidding you joy in the morning.

For ere one half of the night was gone,
Sudden a star has led us on,
Raining bliss and benison—
Bliss tomorrow and more anon,
Joy for every morning.

Good man Joseph toiled through the snow
Saw the star o'er the stable low;
Mary she might not farther go
Welcome thatch and litter below!
Joy was hers in the morning.

And then they heard the angels tell,
"Who were the first to cry noel?
Animals all as it befell,
In the stable where they did dwell!
Joy shall be theirs in the morning."

—KENNETH GRAHAME

A QUIET KNOWING CHRISTMAS

INN

Trouble at the Inn

For years now, whenever Christmas pageants are talked about in a certain little town in the Midwest, someone is sure to mention the name of Wallace Purling. Wally's performance in one annual production of the Nativity play has slipped into the realm of legend. But the old-timers who were in the audience that night never tire of recalling exactly what happened.

Wally was nine that year and in the second grade, though he should have been in the fourth. Most people in town knew that he had difficulty in keeping up. He was big and clumsy, slow in movement and mind. Still, Wally was well liked by the other children in his class, all of whom were smaller than he, though the boys had trouble hiding their irritation when the uncoordinated Wally would ask to play ball with them.

Most often they'd find a way to keep him off the field, but Wally would hang around anyway—not sulking, just hoping. He was always a helpful boy, a willing and smiling one, and the natural protector, paradoxically, of the underdog. Sometimes if the older boys chased the younger ones away, it would always be Wally who'd say, "Can't they stay? They're no bother."

Wally fancied the idea of being a shepherd with a flute in the Christmas pageant that year, but the play's director, Miss Lumbard, assigned him to a more important role. After all, she reasoned, the Innkeeper did not have too many lines, and Wally's size would make his refusal of lodging to Joseph more forceful.

And so it happened that the usual large, partisan audience gathered for the town's Yuletide extravaganza of the crooks and crèches, of beards, crowns, halos, and a whole stageful of squeaky voices. No one on stage or off was more caught up in the magic of the night than Wallace Purling. They said later that he stood in the wings and watched the performance with such fascination that from time to time Miss Lumbard had to make sure he didn't wander onstage before his cue.

Then the time came when Joseph appeared, slowly, tenderly guiding Mary to the door of the inn. Joseph knocked hard on the wooden door set into the painted backdrop. Wally the Innkeeper was there, waiting.

"What do you want?" Wally said, swinging the door open with a brusque gesture.

"We seek lodging."

"Seek it elsewhere." Wally looked straight ahead but spoke vigorously. "The inn is filled."

"Sir, we have asked everywhere in vain. We have traveled far and are very weary."

"There is no room in this inn for you." Wally looked properly stern.

"Please, good innkeeper, this is my wife, Mary. She is heavy with child and needs a place to rest. Surely you must have some small corner for her. She is so tired."

Now for the first time, the Innkeeper relaxed his stiff stance and looked down at Mary. With that, there was a long pause, long enough to make the audience a bit tense with embarrassment.

"No! Be gone!" the prompter whispered from the wings.

"No!" Wally repeated automatically. "Be gone!"

Joseph sadly placed his arm around Mary, and Mary laid her head upon her husband's shoulder and the two of them started to move away. The Innkeeper did not return inside his inn, however. Wally stood there in the doorway, watching the forlorn couple. His mouth was open, his brow creased with concern, his eyes filling unmistakably with tears.

And suddenly this Christmas pageant became different from all others.

"Don't go, Joseph," Wally called out. "Bring Mary back." And Wallace Purling's face grew into a bright smile. "You can have my room."

Some people in town thought that the pageant had been ruined. Yet there were others—many, many others—who considered it the most Christmas of all Christmas pageants they had ever seen.

—DINA DONAHUE
FROM *GUIDEPOSTS, 1966*

PRAYER

Loving Father, help us remember the birth of Jesus,
that we may share in the song of the angels,
the gladness of the shepherds, and the worship of the wise men.
Close the door of hate and open the door of love all over the world.
Let kindness come with every gift and good desires with every greeting.
Deliver us from evil by the blessing which Christ brings,
and teach us to be merry with clear hearts.
May the Christmas morning make us happy to be Thy children,
and the Christmas evening bring us to our beds with grateful thoughts,
forgiving and forgiven, for Jesus' sake. Amen!

—ROBERT LOUIS STEVENSON

A Sheaf of Oats

One of the few traditional Christmas customs that today's Norwegians practice in its original form is that of erecting a julenek, or sheaf of grain for the birds. Equally widespread in both urban and rural areas, the tradition probably survives because it found a place in national romantic artists' depictions of an idealized Norwegian Christmas, and because it adapted easily to modern building styles.

Origins of the custom, however, remain obscure. One of the oldest known descriptions dates only as far back as 1753 and is attributed to Erik Pontoppidan, a prominent clergyman and author of the Forklafing (the explanation of Luther's Small Catechism, which all Norwegians once had to memorize before they could be confirmed). He saw the julenek custom as the "Norwegian peasant's hospitality extending to the birds which he invites to be his guests by placing an unthreshed sheaf of grain on a pole above the barn door." The very next year, however, another minister railed against the identical custom that Pontoppidan had found so charming, decrying it in his Christmas sermon as "one of the most superstitious and therefore sinful practices." This protest—possibly derived from an association of the julenek with the age-old folk belief in grain's power to ward off the supernatural—has led some scholars to think the custom had a pagan origin. Still others see a closer link between this gift of grain and the sense of Christian charity that motivated the commonly taken precaution to keep birds and other animals from being caught in animal traps and snares during the Christmas season. No matter what its origins, the julenek has become a symbol of Christmas generosity and commonly appears on Norwegian Christmas cards, wrapping paper, and gift tags.

—KATHLEEN STOKKER
FROM *KEEPING CHRISTMAS: YULETIDE TRADITIONS
IN NORWAY AND THE NEW LAND*

S W E E T S O U P

*T*he Norwegian-American family's Christmas dinner had its basis in Norwegian models, deriving as in the Old Country from a seasonal abundance of food: "At Christmas time we had ample food resources for the finest of Christmas feasts. Traditional Norwegian delicacies remained at its core, but also includes distinctly American dishes."

The meal begins with sotsuppe (sweet soup), "which had been simmering on the back of the stove all afternoon." It was served every Christmas and consisted of sago, raisins, currants, prunes, lemon peel, spices, and sugar. Most Norwegian Americans, consider sotsuppe "traditional."

There are probably as many variations on sotsuppe as there are cooks who make it.

— K ATHLEEN S TOKKER
FROM *K EEPING C HRISTMAS :*
Y ULETIDE T RADITIONS IN N ORWAY AND THE N EW L AND

Sotsuppe

4 cups water

2 cups grape juice

2 cups raisins

2 cups golden raisins or currants

(Arlene substituted apricots)

1 cup prunes

1 tablespoon lemon juice

(or ½ lemon, sliced)

½ to ⅔ cup sugar

¼ teaspoon salt

2 cinnamon sticks

5 tablespoons quick-cooking tapioca

Bring all ingredients except the tapioca to a boil; reduce heat and simmer 20 minutes or until fruit is tender. Gradually stir in the tapioca and simmer about 15 minutes more.

(Some cooks do not add the grape juice until this point; they then let the soup simmer another 15 minutes.) Serve warm or cold. Arlene served the sotsuppe sprinkled with cinnamon and sugar; some top it with whipped cream.

—ARLENE BRUMBERG AND
DIANE HOUSE

CHAPTER TEN

What Child Is This?

WHAT CHILD IS THIS?

What child is this, who laid to rest
On Mary's lap is sleeping?
Whom angels greet with anthems sweet,
While shepherds watch are keeping?

This, this is Christ the King:
Whom shepherds guard and angels sing:
Haste, haste to bring him laud
The babe, the son of Mary!

Why lies he in such mean estate
Where ox and ass are feeding?
Good Christian, fear, for sinners here
The silent word is pleading.

Nails, spear shall pierce him through,
The cross be borne, for me, for you:
Hail, hail, the word made flesh,
The babe, the son of Mary!

So bring him incense, gold and myrrh,
Come peasant, king to own him,
The king of kings salvation brings,
Let loving hearts enthrone him.

Raise, raise the song on high,
The virgin sings her lullaby:
Joy, joy, for Christ is born,
The babe, the son of Mary!

—LYRIC BY WILLIAM DIX
TRADITIONAL ENGLISH MELODY, "GREENSLEEVES"

The Story of "What Child Is This?"

The question posed in this well-loved carol must have been uppermost in the minds of those present at Jesus' birth. We can almost hear the question being asked from one to another as they gazed into the humble manger. How difficult it must have been for them to understand that the Babe who lay in "such mean estate" was truly the long-awaited Messiah. And through the centuries men have continued to ponder who Christ really is—how can He be fully God and still fully man? Only through divine faith comes the revealed answer.

He who is the Bread of Life began His ministry hungering.
He who is the Water of Life ended His ministry thirsty.
Christ hungered as man, yet fed the multitudes as God.
He was weary, yet He is our rest.
He prayed, yet He hears our prayers.
He was sold for thirty pieces of silver, yet He redeems sinners.
He was led as a lamb to the slaughter, yet He is the Good Shepherd.
He died, and by dying destroyed death.

— AUTHOR UNKNOWN

How forcefully the triumphant answer to this imposing question bursts forth in the refrain "This, this is Christ the King."

This thoughtful text was written by William C. Dix, who was one of our finest lay hymn writers. As a successful insurance administrator in Glasgow, Scotland, he was stricken with a sudden serious illness at the age of twenty-nine. Dix was confined to bed for an extended period and suffered deep depression until he called out to God and "met Him in a new and real way." Out of this spiritual experience came more than forty artistic and distinctive hymns, including this delightful carol. It was taken from a longer Christmas poem, "The Manger Throne," written by Dix in 1865. He based this poem on the nativity account recorded in Matthew 2:1–12. Another well-known text by William Dix is the hymn "As with Gladness Men of Old." It is used especially during the Epiphany season, which begins January 6.

The melody "Greensleeves" is a traditional English folk tune of unknown origin. Through the years it has been associated with a great variety of texts. William Shakespeare noted in some of his plays that "Greensleeves" was a favorite tune of his day.

—Kenneth Osbeck
from *Joy to the World:*
The Stories Behind Your Favorite Christmas Carols

What is the Christmas Spirit?

It is the spirit which brings a smile to the lips and tenderness to the heart; it is the spirit which warms one into friendship with all the world, which impels one to hold out the hand of fellowship to every man and woman.

For the Christmas motto is "Peace on earth, goodwill to men," and the spirit of Christmas demands that it ring in our hearts and find expression in kindly acts and loving words.

What a joyful thing for the world it would be if the Christmas spirit could do this, not only on that holiday, but on every day of the year. What a beautiful place the world would be to live in! Peace and goodwill everywhere and always! Let each one of us resolve that, so far as we are concerned, peace and goodwill shall be our motor every day, and that we will do our best to make the Christmas spirit last all year round.

—Anonymous

A QUIET KNOWING CHRISTMAS

The First Christmas Crib

The following account I have freely translated from the original Latin by the chronicler of the life of Francis, Thomas Da Celano, who lived from 1229 to 1257. It tells the story of how we came to have representations of the Nativity in our homes and churches and public places at Christmastime. The story itself can be more charmingly narrated without the confines of Celano's account. But many believe the story to be an unsubstantiated legend, so by going back to the source of the story it may be proved to be not a legend, but a true account.

With reverential memory we recall that three years before his [Francis's] glorious death what he did on the feast of the birth of our Lord Jesus Christ.

—MARIA HUBERT

There was living in the land a man named John, of meritorious life, whom Francis loved for his noble and honorable ways and spirit. Fifteen days before Christmas he went to this man and said, "If you like we can present, for this Feast, in memory of the Child who was born in Bethlehem, a representation of the uncomfortable way he came into the world, laid in a manger with an ass and an ox nearby."

Francis wanted the people to prepare more diligently for the Coming of Christ at Christmas, by showing them what it must have been like on that first Christmas night in a lowly stable at Bethlehem. He wanted to bring Bethlehem to Grecchio, Italy. He created a manger, and brought an ox and a donkey to the place where he was to celebrate the Christmas Mass.

The night was illuminated like day and men and animals came to the new mystery. The air resounded with silver voices, and jubilant responses. The holy brothers sang praises to God; the whole night resulted in jubilation. He celebrated the solemn Mass over the manger, and enjoyed once more the consolation of his priesthood.

Francis began to tell the story of the first Nativity. He described the place of the nativity in Bethlehem as he himself had seen it when some years earlier he spent time in the Holy Land, and made friends with the great Saladin, who respected the humble friar as he respected no other "Infidel." It was said that the sermon which Francis gave to the people of Grecchio on the hillside that night, illuminated by the torches they carried, was so eloquent that many believed they saw the Baby Jesus in the manger.

After the death of St. Francis, the friars consecrated an altar on the spot where he had brought the story of the Nativity alive on that special night. Shortly afterwards, it became popular to have a representation of the Holy Family in the churches at Christmastime.

Later the wealthy began to have figures made for their homes, and the custom spread with the Franciscan friars as they traveled the world with their missionary zeal.

One of the oldest sets of Nativity figures belonged to Queen Elizabeth of Hungary, herself a Franciscan. It is in the convent of the Poor Clare Nuns in Krakow, Poland, where she ended her days in the thirteenth century.

Italians are still among the best and most famous crib-makers in the world, and at Christmastime, the Christmas markets are full of little figures, which people collect to add to their family Nativity set, making it larger each year or generation.

—COMPILED BY MARIA HUBERT
FROM *CHRISTMAS AROUND THE WORLD*

If You're Missing Baby Jesus, Call 7162

When I was a child, my father worked for an oil company in North Dakota. The company moved him around to different parts of the state and at some point between one move and another, we lost our family nativity set. Shortly before Christmas in 1943, my mother decided to replace it and was happy to find another at our local five and dime for only $3.99. When my brother Tom and I helped her unpack the set, we discovered two figures of the Baby Jesus.

"Someone must have packaged this wrong," my mother said, counting out the figures. "We have one Joseph, one Mary, three wise men, three shepherds, two lambs, a donkey, a cow, an angel, and two babies. Oh, dear! I suppose some set down at the store is missing a Baby Jesus."

"Hey, that's great, Mom," my brother and I shouted. "Now we have twins!"

"You two run back down to the store and tell the manager that we have an extra Jesus. Tell him to put a sign on the remaining boxes saying that if a set is missing a Baby Jesus, call 7162," my mother instructed. "I'll give each of you a penny for some candy. And don't forget your mufflers. It's freezing cold out there."

The manager of the store copied down my mother's message and the next time we were in the store we saw the cardboard sign that read, "If you're missing Baby Jesus, call 7162."

All week long we waited for the call to come. Surely, we thought, someone was missing the important figurine. Each time the phone rang, my mother would say, "I'll bet that's about Jesus," but it never was. My father tried to explain that the figurine could be missing from a set in Walla Walla, Washington, and that packing errors occurred all the time. He suggested we just put the extra Jesus back in the box and forget about it.

"Back in the box!" I wailed. "What a terrible thing to do to the Baby Jesus. And at Christmastime, too."

"Surely someone will call," my mother said. "We'll just keep them together in the manger until someone calls."

When no call had come by 5:00 on Christmas Eve, my mother insisted that my father "just run down to the store" to see if there were any sets left. "You can see them right through the window, over on the counter," she said. "If they are all gone, I'll know someone is bound to call tonight."

"Run down to the store?" my father thundered. "It's fifteen degrees below zero out there!"

"Oh, Daddy, we'll go with you," I said. "Tommy and I will bundle up good. And we can look at all the decorations on the way."

My father gave a long sigh and headed for the front closet. "I can't believe I'm doing this," he muttered. "Each time the phone rings everyone yells at me to see if it's about Jesus, and now I'm going off on the coldest night of the year to peek in a window to see if He's there or not there."

My father muttered all the way down the block while my brother and I raced each other up to the window where the tiny lights flickered on and off around the frame. "They're all gone, Daddy," I shouted. "Every set must be sold."

"Hooray, hooray!" my brother joined in, catching up with me. "The mystery will be solved tonight!"

My father, who had remained several steps behind us, turned on his heel and headed back home.

Inside the house once more, we saw that the extra figurine had vanished from the set and my mother appeared to have vanished, too. "Someone must have called and she went out to deliver the figurine," my father reasoned, pulling off his boots. "You kids get busy stringing popcorn strands for the tree and I'll wrap your mother's present."

We had almost completed one strand when the phone rang. My father yelled for me to answer it. "Tell 'em we found a home for Jesus," he called down the steps. But the caller was not an inquirer. It was my mother with instructions for us to come to 205 Chestnut Street immediately and bring three blankets, a box of cookies, and some milk.

"Now what has she gotten us into?" my father groaned as we bundled up again. "205 Chestnut Street. Why, that's about eight blocks away. Wrap that milk up good in the blankets or it will turn to ice by the time we get there. Why in the name of heaven can't we all just get on with Christmas? It's probably twenty degrees below out there now. And the wind is picking up. Of all the crazy things to do on a night like this."

Tommy and I sang Christmas songs at the top of our lungs all the way to Chestnut Street. My father, carrying his bundle of blankets and milk, looked for all the world like Nicholas himself with his arms full of goodies. Every now and then my brother would call back to him, "Let's pretend we're looking for a place to stay, Dad, just like Joseph and Mary."

"Let's pretend we are in Bethlehem where it is probably sixty-five degrees in the shade right now," my father would answer.

The house at 205 Chestnut Street turned out to be

the darkest one on the block. One tiny light burned in the living room and the moment we set foot on the porch steps, my mother opened the door and shouted, "They're here, they're here. Oh, thank God you got here, Ray! You kids take those blankets into the living room and wrap up the little ones on the couch. I'll take the milk and cookies."

"Would you mind telling me what is going on, Ethel?" my father asked. "We have just walked through below zero weather with the wind in our faces all the way."

"Never mind all that now," my mother interrupted. "There is no heat in this house and this young mother is so upset she doesn't know what to do. Her husband walked out on her and those poor children will have to spend a very bleak Christmas, so don't you complain. I told her you could fix that oil furnace in a jiffy."

My mother strode off to the kitchen to warm the milk while my brother and I wrapped up the five little children who were huddled together on the couch. The children's mother explained to my father that her husband had run off, taking bedding, clothing, and almost every piece of furniture, but she had been doing all right until the furnace broke down.

"I been doin' washin' and ironin' for people and cleanin' the five and dime," she said. "I saw your number every day there, on those boxes on the counter. When the furnace went out, that number kept goin' through my mind: 7162 . . . 7162.

"Said on the box that if a person was missin' Jesus, they should call you. That's how I knew you were good Christian people, willin' to help folks. I figured that maybe you would help me, too. So I stopped at the grocery store tonight and I called your missus. I'm not missin' Jesus, mister, because I sure love the Lord. But I am missin' heat.

"Me and the kids ain't got no beddin', no warm clothes. I got a few Christmas toys for them, but I got no money to fix that furnace."

"Okay, okay," my father said kindly. "You've come to the right place. Now let's see. You've got a little oil burner over there in the dining room. Shouldn't be too hard to fix. Probably just a clogged flue. I'll look it over, see what it needs."

My mother came into the living room carrying a plate of cookies and a tray with warm milk. As she set the cups down on the coffee table, I noticed the figure of the Baby Jesus lying in the center of the table. It was the only sign of the Christmas season in the house. The children stared wide-eyed with wonder at the plate of cookies my mother set before them. One of the littlest ones woke up and crawled out from under the blanket. Seeing all the strangers in his house, he began to cry. My mother swooped him up in her arms and began to sing to him.

"This, this, is Christ the King, Whom shepherds guard and angels sing," she crooned while the child wailed.

"Haste, haste to bring Him laud, the Babe, the son of Mary," she sang, oblivious to the child's cries. She sang and danced the baby around the room until he settled down again.

"You hear that, Chester?" the young mother said to another child. "That woman is sin-gin' 'bout the Lord Jesus. He ain't ever gonna walk out on us. Why, He sent these people to us just to fix our furnace. And blankets we got now, too. Oh, we'll be warm tonight."

My father, finishing his work on the oil burner, wiped his hands on his muffler and said, "I've got it going, but you need more oil. I'll make a few calls tonight when I get home and we'll get you some oil. Yessir, you came to the right place," he grinned.

When my father calculated that the furnace was going strong once more, our family bundled up and made our way home. My father didn't say a thing about the cold weather and had barely set foot inside the front door when he was on the phone.

"Ed, hey, how are ya, Ed?" I heard him say. "Yes, Merry Christmas to you, too. Say Ed, we have kind of an unusual situation here and I know you've got that pick-up truck. I wonder if we could round up some of the boys and find a Christmas tree, you know, and a couple of things for . . ."

The rest of his conversation was lost in a blur of words as my brother and I ran to our rooms and began pulling clothes out of our closets and toys off of our shelves. My mother checked through our belongings for sizes and games she said "might do" and added some of her own sweaters and slacks to our stack. We were up way past our bedtime that night wrapping our gifts. The men my father had called found oil for the furnace, bedding, two chairs, three lamps and had made two trips to 205 Chestnut before the night was done. Our gifts were piled into the truck on the second trip, and even though it must have been thirty degrees below by then, my father let us ride along in the back of the truck.

No one ever did call about the missing figurine in the nativity set, but as I grow older I realize that it wasn't a packing mistake at all.

—JEAN GIETZEN
FROM *VIRTUE*, NOV/DEC 1983

Manger Haystacks

1 3-ounce package cream cheese

2 tablespoons milk

3 cups confectioners sugar

2 1-ounce squares unsweetened
chocolate, melted

1/4 teaspoon vanilla

1/2 cup chopped nuts

dash of salt

3 cups small marshmallows

flaked coconut

Combine softened cream cheese
and milk. Mix well. Gradually add
sugar. Stir in chocolate, vanilla,
nuts, and salt. Fold in marshmallows. Drop rounded teaspoons of
mixture into coconut. Toss until
well covered. Chill.

Dove of Peace

Throughout time, the dove has meant peace. This easy-to-make dove is one youngsters as well as adults will have fun making.

MATERIALS: heavyweight construction paper, household cement, thin gold cord

DIRECTIONS: Trace one dove body, two crowns, two wings, and two body strips onto the construction paper. Crease the wings and the body strips according to the folds you find on each of the pattern pieces.

Glue the pieces to each side of the body with household cement.

String from the tree with thin gold cord.

147

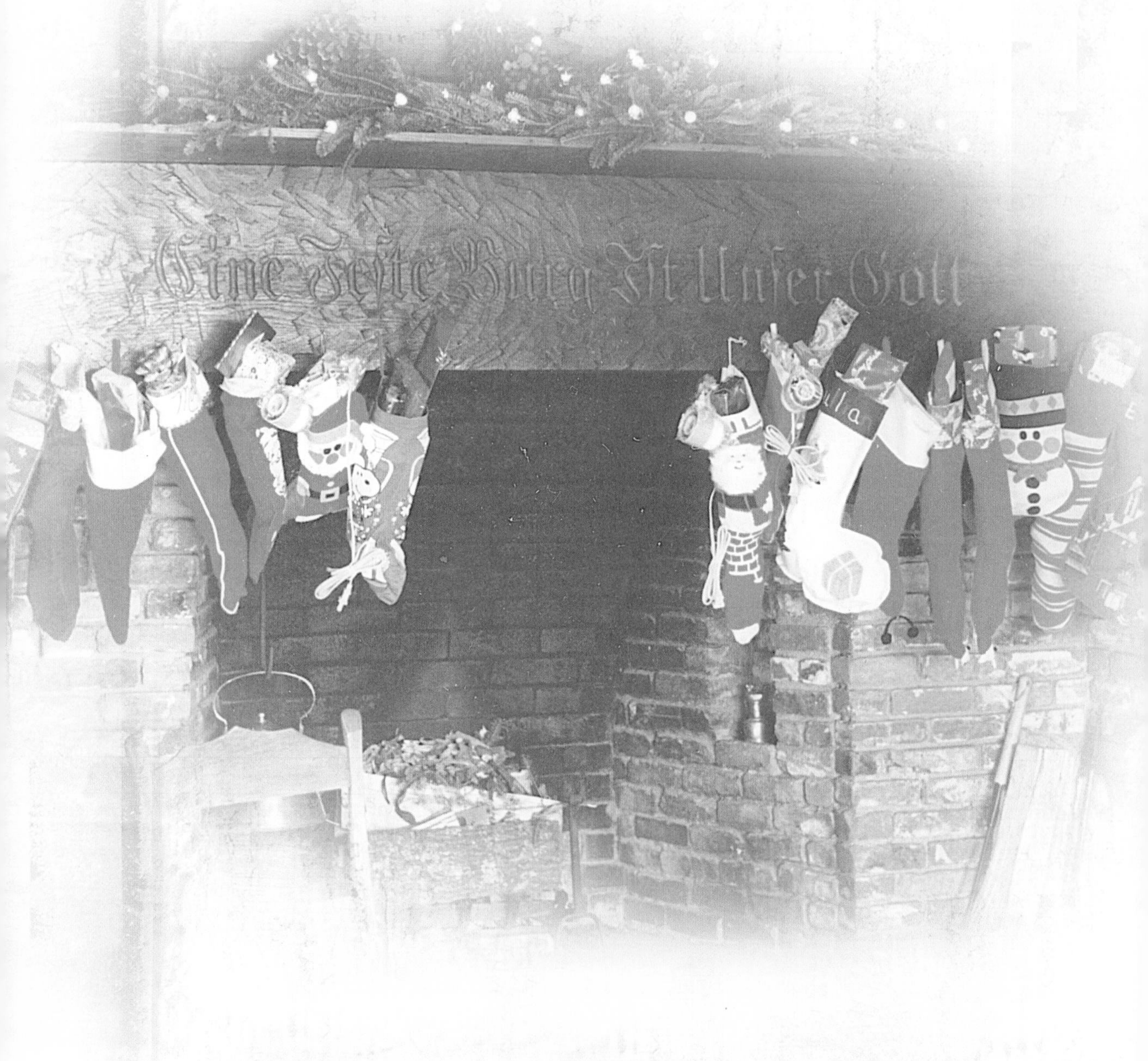
Eine Feste Burg Ist Unser Gott

CHAPTER ELEVEN

O Come, O Come, Emmanuel

O Come, O Come, Emmanuel

O come, O come, Emmanuel,
And ransom captive Israel,
That mourns in lowly exile here,
Until the Son of God appear
Rejoice! Rejoice! Emmanuel
Shall come to thee, O Israel.

O Come, thou rod of Jesse, free
Thine own from Satan's tyranny;
From depths of hell thy people save,
And give them vict'ry o'er the grave.
Rejoice! Rejoice! Emmanuel
Shall come to thee, O Israel.

O come, thou Day-spring from on high
And cheer us by thy drawing nigh;
Disperse the gloomy clouds of night,
And death's dark shadows put to flight.
Rejoice! Rejoice! Emmanuel
Shall come to thee, O Israel.

O come, thou Key of David, come
And open wide our heav'nly home;
Disperse the gloomy clouds of night,
And close the path to misery.
Rejoice! Rejoice! Emmanuel
Shall come to thee, O Israel.

—Twelfth-Century Latin Hymn, Trans. by John Mason Neale, 1851
Ancient Plainsong, Thirteenth-Century

The Story of
"O Come, O Come, Emmanuel"

*T*he preparation for the celebration of our Lord's birth begins four Sundays before Christmas Day, a period known as the Advent season. The traditional church color for this season is purple, symbolic of the promised Messiah's royalty. Many churches, as well as Christian families, observe and prepare for Christ's birth by lighting a new candle on each of the four Sundays preceding Christmas Day.

The Advent season centers on the Old Testament prophecies concerning a coming Messiah-Deliverer. The Messiah's promised coming was foretold seven centuries before Christ's birth. At the time, the Jewish people were living in captivity in Babylon. For generations thereafter, faithful Israelites earnestly anticipated their Messiah with great longing and expectation, echoing the prayer that He would "ransom captive Israel." Perhaps the bleakest period in Israel's history was the time of the four hundred silent years between the close of the Book of Malachi and the opening of the Gospel of Matthew. The Jewish hope of a promised Messiah was all but lost in times of extreme cruelty and destruction dealt to the Jewish people by such enemies as the Egyptians, the Syrians, and the Romans. But finally the long-awaited heavenly announcement came: "Unto you is born this day in the city of David a Saviour, which is Christ the Lord" (Luke 2:11).

The tragedy of tragedies, however, is the biblical truth that the Messiah came to His own people to establish a spiritual kingdom of both redeemed Jews and Gentiles, but His own people rejected Him. The good news is that citizenship in God's kingdom became available to all who respond with personal faith to the redemptive work of His Son, our Messiah, Savior.

"O Come, O Come, Emmanuel" was originally used in the medieval church liturgy as a series of antiphon—short musical statements that were sung for the vesper services during the Advent season. Each of these antiphons greets the anticipated Messiah with one of the titles ascribed to Him throughout the Old Testament: Wisdom, Emmanuel, the Lord of Might, the Rod of Jesse, Day-Spring, and the Key of David.

The translation of this hymn from Latin to English did not occur until the nineteenth century. It was done by John Neale, a humble but brilliant Anglican pastor and scholar. The haunting modal melody for the verses is also of ancient origin. It is based on one of the earliest known forms of sacred music—the chant or plainsong.

FROM *JOY TO THE WORLD:*
THE STORIES BEHIND YOUR FAVORITE CHRISTMAS CAROLS

There's No Such Thing As a Poor Christmas

My mother, Muv, once made dumplings to go with three cans of Vienna sausage for Thanksgiving dinner.

If you've ever bought Vienna sausage for seven cents a can at a sawmill–turpentine still commissary, you will understand the significance of that.

It bespeaks a woman of imagination. Who else would think the union of Vienna sausage and dumplings possible, much less feasible? More important, it indicates an unquenchable zest for celebration.

Muv believes that you should put everything you have and everything you can get into an important occasion. We had the Vienna sausage—and very little else in those Depression years of the 1930s. She made the dumplings.

When I think of that Thanksgiving dinner, served out of the Sunday dishes, on the very best tablecloth, with a fire burning brightly on the hearth and a bowlful of apples our cousin sent from Virginia polished to a high sheen for a centerpiece, I wouldn't dare question Muv's convictions about Christmas.

For if Thanksgiving is important—and oh, it is!—how much more important is Christmas. Anybody who would po'mouth Christmas, contends my mother, is guilty of sinning against both heaven and his fellowman. He's a hangdog, mean-spirited character who is unworthy of receiving the greatest Gift of all time.

My father, reared a Scotch Presbyterian with a more moderate (Muv would say tepid) approach to most things, may have once regarded Muv's feelings about Christmas as a bit extravagant. But early in their marriage she beat him into line with weapons he normally handled best—ethical and spiritual arguments.

He made the mistake one grayish December morning of observing bleakly that the lumber business was going badly and "it looks like a poor Christmas this year."

"A poor Christmas!" cried Muv. "Shame on you! There's no such thing as a poor Christmas!"

Poor people and hard times, yes. They were not new in Christ's time and they were certainly not new in rural Alabama. But no matter what you had or didn't have in a material way, Christmas stood by itself—glorious and unmatched by anything else that had happened in the history of the world. Jesus himself had come to dwell among men, and with a richness like that to celebrate, who could be so meaching and self-centered as to speak of a "poor" Christmas?

"Make a joyful noise unto the Lord!" directed Muv gustily, and if my father found he couldn't do that, he at least didn't grouse. He was to learn later that he didn't dare to even look unjoyful about the approach of Christmas, or Muv would do something wild and unprecedented to cheer him up, like the year she took tailoring lessons and made him a new suit and topped it off by buying him a pearl stickpin at a $1-down-and-charge jewelry store.

The suit was beautifully made and a perfect fit and Muv had even worked out the cost of the goods by helping the tailor, but I think it made my father a little uneasy to be so splendidly arrayed at a time when he had come to accept, even to take pride in the image of himself as a "poor man." And the idea of owing for something as frivolous as a piece of jewelry was so repugnant to him that he finished paying for the stickpin himself. But he loved having it, wore it with pleasure, and thereafter looked at Muv and the ardor which she poured into preparations for Christmas with a touch of awe.

Things aren't important, people are, Muv preached, and it sounded so fine it was years before I realized what she meant to us. Things weren't important to us, so as fast as gift packages came in from distant kin, Muv unwrapped them, admired them and with a gleam in her eye that I came to dread said happily, "Now who can we give this to?"

It's funny that with the passage of the years only one or two of the Things stand out in memory. There were some lavender garters a boy in the sixth grade gave me. ("Beautiful!" said Muv. "You can give them to Aunt Sister!") And there was a green crepe de chine dress I think I still mourn for a little bit. ("Oh, it's so pretty! Don't you want to give it to Julia Belle?")

Julia Belle was a skinny little Negro girl in the quarters who had lost her baby in a fire and kept wandering up and down the road wringing her hands and crying. My green dress was such a dazzling gift, it did divert her from her grief a little, and it may have helped her along the road to recovery.

At the time, I remember protesting that I loved the dress and wanted it myself and Muv said blithely, "Of course you do. It's no gift if it's something you don't care about!"

It must be true because the other Things are lost to memory, but the People remain. Through the years there have been a lot of them, disreputable, distinguished, outrageous, inspiring, and at Christmastime I remember them and the gifts they gave to me— the gifts, in fact, that they were.

—CELESTINE SIBLEY
FROM *ESPECIALLY AT CHRISTMAS*

A QUIET KNOWING CHRISTMAS

A CONCLUSION

For God So Loved the World

The Tree

I clutched my shawl around me. The night air in Jerusalem can be chilly, especially in December.

Standing on the balcony of our apartment, I watched the stars twinkling against the ebony sky and couldn't help wondering if the sky looked something like this on the night Jesus was born.

I glanced in the direction of Bethlehem, only a few miles away. Somehow, it just didn't seem much like Christmas. No bright lights dangling from street corners. No Christmas carols blaring from the radio. No Santas in red suits. No Salvation Army bell ringers. Except for the busloads of tourists stopping to view the traditional nativity site, there was scant evidence of the celebration of the birth of Christ.

I surveyed the hills around me. In each window of the apartment buildings dotting the landscape, Hanukkah candles gave off a soft glow. Happy sounds of Israeli families celebrating the Festival of Lights drifted across the valley, a painful reminder of how much I missed my own family, thousands of miles away. Soon, they would be gathering around the open fireplace, singing carols, and exchanging the gaily wrapped gifts placed under the Christmas tree.

I thought of our apartment where Stephan and I lived, bare and devoid of all but a few signs that Christmas was only days away. Here in Israel, it wasn't possible to purchase a Christmas tree. Nor could we go into the surrounding hills and cut one

down that had been so lovingly planted by Jews from around the world in the successful land reclamation program.

I sighed and turned to go in. Glancing once more at the heavens, I breathed a
quick prayer.

"Lord . . . please make this holy season in this ancient place—this place You visited
so long ago—something special this year."

The next day, as we left our apartment to do some errands, our Jewish neighbors
came running across the parking lot to meet us.

"Would you like a Christmas tree?" they asked.

A Christmas tree? I had trouble believing my ears.

We assured them we would love to have a tree, but didn't know of anyplace to buy one.

"Oh, you don't have to buy it," they answered. "We've heard that on December 22,
in the center of town, trees will be given away. Knowing that you are Christians, we
thought you might like to have one."

We warmly thanked our neighbors, and on the designated day we went to see about
this strange phenomenon . . . a Christmas tree lot in Israel!

Somehow, it was true. We selected a lovely evergreen and placed it in the trunk,
hoping no one would think we had cut it down. As we unloaded it at our apartment, we
noticed the tag attached to the tree: "Compliments of the Jewish Tourist Agency."

Collecting ornaments was like a scavenger hunt. We found a string of lights in a
dusty corner of a department store, a few bright balls in another. We popped popcorn
and lit candles. And it was beginning to look a lot like Christmas.

As I hung the ornaments and strung the popcorn, I reflected on the spiritual heritage
this little country had given me. As much as I longed to see my family, as much as I
missed the familiar mountains of home, my true roots were not so much in the soil of
North Carolina as here . . . in Israel . . . in Bethlehem.

Since childhood I had been acquainted with the geography and history of this land.

I smiled to myself, suddenly realizing I knew more names of ancient cities and towns here in Israel than I did in North Carolina.

I climbed up on a chair to rearrange an errant string of popcorn. I thought, *If only those who live in this land could know that Messiah, the Son of David, has already come. If only they could realize that Jesus was either a liar, an egomaniac making wild and crazy claims, or that He is who He claimed to be . . . the very Son of God.*

I climbed down and stepped back to examine my work. As I stood there admiring our little tree, I suddenly realized just how significant the tree is in the Christmas story. It reminds us not only of Bethlehem, but also of Calvary.

"For God so loved the world that He gave His only Son."

Jesus was born for the expressed purpose of going from the cradle to the cross. For me. For us all.

My prayer had been answered. The tree had focused my attention on the significant, causing this Christmas to be very special. Yes, we had less. Less gifts. Less decorations. Less family. Less distractions.

But we also had more. More love and appreciation. More time and perspective to weigh the true meaning of Christmas. More to cherish and adore. More of Him.

—GIGI GRAHAM TCHIVIDJIAN

THERE WILL BE LESS SOMEDAY

There will be less someday—
much less,
and there will be More;
less to distract and amuse;
More to adore
less to burden and confuse
More, to undo
the cluttering of centuries,
that we might view again,
That which star and angels pointed to;
we shall be poorer—
and richer;
stripped—and free:
for always there will be a Gift
always a Tree.

—RUTH BELL GRAHAM
FROM *RUTH BELL GRAHAM'S COLLECTED POEMS*

Immanuel

"They will call him Immanuel"—which means, "God with us."
—MATTHEW 1:23 NIV

It was a real shopper stopper of a choir. My family and I had joined the teeming crowds shopping at the local mall on the day after Thanksgiving. My older children and their mother had departed on various secret missions leaving me alone to occupy the attention of our two-year-old. It wasn't so hard—at first. There were plenty of store windows, toy displays, and bustling people sights to fascinate children of all ages.

Eventually and inevitably, however, my little girl began to wear out (or maybe I was simply wearing down). We sat for rest in the center courtyard of the mall where a church choir had gathered to sing amid the entire consumer overload.

"Now this," I thought as I drifted into my sermon-musing mode, "is a wonderful Christmas metaphor—wedged into a small crack of our self-indulgence, material frenzy, and harried attempts to find happiness in what we can buy is this choral proclamation of Jesus. This is just too good to ignore. I can use this as a sermon illustration."

The choir really was good, too. It was so good that a number of shoppers really did stop to listen. I liked the way that this illustration was developing.

Then the illustration soured a bit when I realized that the video cams and flash cameras among those listening indicated most onlookers were related to the choir.

Perhaps only a dozen persons out of the thousands shopping actually did turn from their present pursuits to listen despite the excellence of the music and the beauty of its message. This Christmas metaphor was not quite as good as I had hoped.

The more I looked the worse the metaphor got. The choir really was wedged into the setting. The majority of the courtyard had been taken over by package wrapping tables. Anything you bought at the mall that day, you could have wrapped there free. The package wrappers with their cellophane paper and ribbons had backed the hymn singers into a small corner of the courtyard. No preacher optimism could overlook how far they were from center stage, or from being the center of attention.

Crowded in that corner of the consumer stage, the backdrop of the church choir became equally obvious and distracting. While the carolers sang "God rest you merry gentlemen," two storefronts served as the choir's rear sounding board.

Behind one angle of the stage was Success Unlimited, a store specializing in calendars and posters with snappy slogans proclaiming that you can be infinitely successful so long as you believe enough in yourself. Behind the other angle was a Nature Songs store with its mystical combination of lava lamps, mother earth curios, crystal selections, and New Age music. I noticed with sadness that these background props were getting far more attention and business than the choir in the foreground.

"At least some people are listening," I reasoned, looking to bolster my quickly eroding seasonal cheer. "Even if the audience is small, the choir members' red and green sweatshirts rightly proclaim 'Wise men still seek him.'"

Apparently, at least one wise guy, however, was seeking the choir for other reasons. I had sat with my back against a trash can for a little lumbar support. Suddenly, a group of security officers gathered around me—above and behind—using the top of the trash can to map out how they were going to corner a shoplifter who was trying to disappear among the choir's listeners.

Unfortunately, the security men so focused on their plans that when they looked up, the thief had slipped away. The officers scurried after their prey expressing their embarrassment and frustration in profanity that punctuated the choir's closing verse of "Silent Night, Holy Night."

Is there to be no redeeming feature of this event? I wondered. *Well, at least the message the choir is singing is redemptive.* I really did not mind that their version of "Silent Night" was sung to a disco beat, for I have resolved to be tolerant of worship styles. I still rejoiced at the repeated final words and hoped they still rang true for a few: "Jesus, Lord at thy birth; Jesus, Lord at thy birth." Here at least was some truth among the trauma of my illustration.

Then, in what I am sure someone thought was a masterstroke of the choir's own tolerance, compassion, and political correctness, the choir segued directly from the words "Jesus, Lord at thy birth" to a rousing rendition of "Happy Chanukah."

I got up to leave in frustration and disgust. There really was not going to be any redeeming feature of this event.

But as I rose to go, a plaintive cry rose also . . . from my daughter. Nearly forgotten in my preacher ruminations was the child I was supposed to be watching. All this time she had sat contentedly at my side. She had been at peace amid all the bustle, cussing, and disco. Only now did she cry out, because until that moment she knew that I was with her. For my child, the redeeming aspect of the occasion was something that I had overlooked: Peace was not in what was around her but in who was beside her. I was with her.

I considered the reason for my daughter's comfort in the light of Christ's identification as Immanuel, God with us. Apart from the truth of that title, there is not much to redeem the images upon which we usually focus in celebrating Christmas. All the bright images of the original Advent drama get even more sullied than my illustration.

Angel choirs deserving grandest cathedral glory sing to humble shepherds in open fields.

We witness the culmination of David's royal line—in a stable.

We observe the Holy Child—dressed in strips of discarded cloth.

Natal star brilliance—becomes target light for a pagan king.

The birth of the newborn King—provides excuse for infant slaughter.

The images meant to communicate joy presage disappointment and disaster. Each new detail introduces another cause for frustration and disgust. The more the story progresses, the worse its horror. Is there no redeeming feature of the accounts we hold so dear? The answer comes in the name, Immanuel.

God is with us. This is the great message of the Gospel and the redeeming truth of all the vain pursuits and preempted joys of this season. Despite the darkness of our circumstances and our souls, our God came to be with us.

This truth does not make the world go away. The advent of our God in his creation did not remove all trial, difficulty, or ugliness from our existence, but it did bring peace to those who would experience all these things with the knowledge of Immanuel.

This peace is still ours to celebrate. We mark the physical entry of our Lord into this world during this season, but we measure his continuance by the witness of his spirit in our hearts. This witness enables us still to marvel that he who knows of our sin and weakness would yet come to dwell with us when there is no redeeming feature in us. Even when our frustration and disgust are with ourselves, he promises never to leave us.

As a child can be virtually oblivious to sham and misery about her when her father is with her, so we can be at peace amid our greatest of difficulties when we know Immanuel, God with us.

One of the most striking images of any Christmas was the product of great misery and pain. When captivity of the American hostages in Iran had stretched many months, the terrorists made a small concession to world opinion by allowing the hostages a brief Christmas celebration.

The terrorists videotaped that worship of the Christ child. The most telling image later broadcast around the world was of Katherine Koob singing a children's carol.

Despite the surrounding terrors of machine guns, hostile religion, dark captivity, and an uncertain future, she sang "Away in a Manger." In those circumstances, the last verse was the most poignant and precious: "Be near me, Lord Jesus, I ask thee to stay close by me forever and love me I pray. Bless all the dear children in thy tender care, and fit us for heaven to live with thee there."

The parting petitions of this familiar carol would never be more apt, for when our God is with us, his children find rest amid the ruins of our humanity. In his presence is peace whatever the world's trials, terrors, and temptations. Thus, he gives us the present of irrepressible joy—his very self. He is Immanuel, God with us.

—B R Y A N C H A P E L L

SNOW

Was it a cold awakening Christmas morning
In a wooden trough,
In spite of straw and swaddling clothes and angel songs?
That was not to be the last time
You'd be laid upon the wood
(There were Herods, Judases from the start
Among the stars and shepherds),
And did they smile, those simple folk,
And kiss your tiny hands and weep delight?
They'd touch those hands again someday,
Believing you through cracks and scars.
Then oh! the million Christmas mornings
When you'd lie, a babe again,
Beneath a million million trees
And hear the countless tongues chanting your name.
And oh! the white snow on black shingles
Where icy crystals capture windows
And fires glow and mistletoe is wreathed and strung.
But ah . . . will they remember crimson
Dripping from the iron nails
And will they pray, and will they know
A whiter white than Snow?

—KEITH PATMAN

B I B L I O G R A P H Y

The books below were used in this collection and are highly recommended additions to your library.

Harrison, Michael and Christopher Stuart-Clark, eds. *Bright Star Shining: Poems for Christmas.* Oxford: Oxford University Press, 1993.

Hollander, John and J. D. McClatchy , eds. *Christmas Poems.* New York: Alfred A. Knopf, 1999.

Smith, Lillian. *Memory of a Large Christmas.* Athens, GA: University of Georgia Press, 1961.

The following books were also used in this collection.

Alden, Raymond MacDonald. *Why the Chimes Rang.* New York: The Bobbs-Merrill Company, Inc., 1906.

Bennett, Arnold. *The Feast of St. Friend.* New York: George H. Doran Company, 1911.

Berry, Wendell. "Our Christmas Tree," from *Christmas Poems.* John Hollander and J. D. McClatchy, eds. New York: Knopf, 1999.

Bevilacqua, Michelle and Brandon Toropoo. *The Everything Christmas Book.* Avon, MA: Adams Media Corporation, 1994, 1996.

Boreham, F. W. *My Christmas Book.* Grand Rapids, MI: Zondervan Publishing House, 1953.

Brown, Joan Winmill. *Best of Christmas Joys.* New York: Doubleday-Galilee Books, 1983.

Cannarella, Deborah, ed. *Christmas Treasures.* New York: Beaux Arts Editions, 1998.

Carter, Jimmy. *Christmas in Plains: Memories.* New York: Simon and Schuster, 2001.

Charlton, James and Barbara Gilson, eds. *A Christmas Treasury of Yuletide & Poems.* New York: Galahad Books, 1976.
Christmas Memories with Recipes. New York: Wings Books, 1999.

Chute, Marchette. "Day Before Christmas." From *Treasury of Christmas Stories*, edited by Ann McGovern, ed. New York: Galahad Books, 1960.

Dalgliesh, Alice, ed. *Christmas: A Book of Stories Old and New.* New York: Charles Scribner's Sons, 1934, 1950.

Dickens, Charles. *Household Words.* London: Bradbury & Evans, 1850, 1859.

Dickens, Charles. *Sketches by Boz.* New York: Dutton, 1968.

Edersheim, Alfred. *The Life and Times of Jesus the Messiah.* New York: Longmans, 1904.

Donahue, Dina. "Trouble at the Inn." From *Guideposts, (*1966).

Farm Journal's Country Cookbook (revised and enlarged edition). New York: Doubleday, 1959.

Garland, Hamlin. "My First Christmas Tree." From *Christmas Treasures,* Deborah Cannarella, ed. New York: Beaux Arts Editions, 1998.

Gietzen, Jean. "If You're Missing Baby Jesus, Call 7162." From *Virtue* (Nov/Dec 1983).

Graham, Ruth Bell. *One Wintry Night.* Grand Rapids, MI: Baker Book House, 1994.

Graham, Ruth Bell. "There Will Be Less Some Day" and "Those Were No Ordinary Sheep." From *Ruth Bell Graham's Collected Poems.* Grand Rapids, MI: Baker Book House, 1997.

Grahame, Kenneth. "Christmas Carol." From *Wind in the Willows.* New York: Golden Press, 1968.

Gray, Alice, comp. *Christmas Stories for the Heart.* Sisters, OR: Multnomah Publishers, Inc., 1997, 2000.

Grief, Martin, ed. *The St. Nicholas Book: A Celebration of Christmas Past.* Pittstown, NJ: The Main Street Press, 1986.

Hollander, John and J. D. McClatchy. *Christmas Poems.* New York: Alfred A. Knopf, 1999.

Howells, William Dean. *Christmas Every Day: A Story Told a Child.* New York: Harper & Brothers, 1908.

Hubert, Maria, ed. *Christmas Around the World.* Trowbridge, Wiltshire, UK: Sutton Publishing, 1998.

Karas, Sheryl Ann. *The Solstice Evergreen: The History, Folklore and Origins of the Christmas Tree.* Boulder Creek, CA: Aslan Publishing, 1991.

Lederer, William J. *A Happy Book of Happy Stories.* New York: W. W. Norton & Company, Inc., 1981.

Macy, John. "The True Story of Santy Claus." From *The Fireside Book of Christmas Stories,* Edward Wagenknecht, ed. Indianapolis, IN: Bobbs-Merrill, 1945.

McGovern, Ann, ed. *Treasury of Christmas Stories.* New York: Galahad Books, 1960.

Montgomery, L. M. Rea Wilmshurst, ed. *Christmas with Anne and Other Holiday Stories.* New York: Delacorte Press, 1995.

Nichols, Nell B., ed. *Farm Journal's Country Cookbook.* New York: Doubleday and Company, Inc., 1959, 1972.

Norris, Leslie. *Norris's Ark.* Portsmouth, NH: Tidal Press, 1988.

Osbeck, Kenneth W. *Joy to the World: The Stories Behind Your Favorite Christmas Carols.* Grand Rapids, MI: Kregel Publications, 1999.

Patman, Keith. *Star Like a Lion's Eye: Twelve Poems for the Christmas Season*. Mansfield, OH: Still Point Press, 1980.

Rogers, Dale Evans. *Christmas Is Always*. Old Tappen, NJ: Fleming H. Revell, 1958.

St. John, Patricia M. *Treasures of the Snow: A Story of Switzerland for Children*. London: C. S. S. M., 1950.

Schaeffer, Edith. *What Is A Family?* Grand Rapids, MI: Baker Book House, 1975.

Sibley, Celestine. *Especially at Christmas*. Atlanta, GA: Peachtree Publishers, Ltd., 1985.

Silber, Irwin. *The Season of the Year: Folk Songs of Christmas and the New Year*. New York: Oak Publications, 1971.

Stervenz, Carol Endler and Nancy Johnson, text by Gary Walther. *The Decorated Tree: Re-creating Traditional Christmas Ornaments*. New York: Harry N. Abrams, Inc, 1982.

Stokker, Kathleen. *Keeping Christmas: Yuletide Traditions in Norway and the New Land*. St. Paul, MN: Minnesota Historical Society Press, 2000.

Tchividjian, Gigi Graham. "Bethlehem Was Never As Miserable As This." From *Currents of the Heart*. Sisters, OR: Multnomah Books, 1996.

Tchividjian, Gigi Graham. "The Tree," From *Weatherproof Your Heart*. Grand Rapids, MI: Baker Books, 1991.

Wagenknecht, Edward, ed. *The Fireside Book of Christmas Stories*. New York: The Bobbs-Merrill Company, 1945.

Wheeler, Joe, ed. *Christmas in My Heart: A Timeless Treasury of Heartwarming Stories*. New York: Bantam Doubleday Dell Publishing, 1996.

Wiggin, Kate Douglas. *The Birds' Christmas Carol*. Boston: Houghlin, Mifflin Company, 1941.

World Book Encyclopedia. Chicago, IL: 1991, 1988, 1984, 1978, 1974.

All Recipes and crafts were tested for this book by Alexa and Victoria Griffith.

Other Contributors

Arlene Brumbert and Diane House
Jackie Camby and Ann Sluder
Bryan Chapell
Charlene Dickerson
Lorraine Griffith
Martha Wiebe

The structure and organization of this book reflects the excellent recording *A Quiet Knowing Christmas*. The CD features twelve instrumental renditions of the carols featured in this book.

A Quiet Knowing Christmas Jeff Johnson, Brian Dunning, & John Fitzpatrick AKD-1507 www.arkmusic.com. Toll free ordering: 877-733-8820.

Also, don't miss *A Quiet Knowing—Canticles for the Heart*, featuring the favorite hymns of Ruth Bell Graham. The CD features twelve instrumental renditions of ten traditional and two contemporary hymns containing strong Celtic and Appalachian influences. Songs include: Softly & Tenderly Jesus Is Calling • A Quiet Knowing • Amazing Grace • Great Is Thy Faithfulness • Just As I Am • The Ninety & Nine • Be Thou My Vision • Children Of The Heavenly Father • Jesus Loves Me • Love Divine • Come Ye Sinners • Even If

A Quiet Knowing—Canticles for the Heart Jeff Johnson & Brian Dunning with John Fitzpatrick AKD-1504 www.arkmusic.com. Toll free ordering: 877-733-8820.

Access to many of the stories, anecdotes, quotes, recipes, and decorations in this book were only possible because of the internet and the ease with which out-of-print books can be found. Of the hundreds of Christmas books read to make this collections, many were found through Amazon (amazon.com), Ebay (half.com), Alibris (alibris.com), and Barnes and Noble (bn.com).

We have diligently attempted to locate and obtain permission from the writers or publishers of all materials used in this book. Those credit lines that are received after publication will appear in the next printing and will be posted on the web site: www.ruthbellgraham.com.

"Trouble at the Inn" by Dina Donahue.
Used with permission from Guideposts.
Copyright © 1966 by Guideposts, Carmel, New York 10512.

"Bethlehem Was Never as Miserable as This!" excerpted from *Currents of the Heart* © 1996 by Gigi Graham Tchvidjian.
Used by permission of Multnomah Publishers, Inc.